S O S

POEMS 1961–2013

S O S

Calling black people
Calling all black people, man woman child
Wherever you are, calling you, urgent, come in
Black People, come in, wherever you are, urgent, calling
you, calling all black people
calling all black people, come in, black people, come
on in.

S O S

POEMS 1961–2013

AMIRI BARAKA

SELECTED BY PAUL VANGELISTI

Grove Press
New York

Printed in the United States of America
Published simultaneously in Canada

FIRST EDITION

ISBN 978-0-8021-2335-0
eISBN 978-0-8021-9158-8

Grove Press
an imprint of Grove/Atlantic, Inc.
154 West 14th Street
New York, NY 10011

Distributed by Publishers Group West

www.groveatlantic.com

15 16 17   10 9 8 7 6 5 4 3 2 1

TABLE OF CONTENTS

BLACK MAGIC (1969)

HARD FACTS (1972)

FUNK LORE (1995)

Preface by Paul Vangelisti

S O S traces the almost sixty-year career of a writer who may be, along with Ezra Pound, one of the most important and least understood American poets of the past century. The selection attests to a life's work that is both a body of poetry and a body of knowledge, passionate, often self-critical reflections on the culture and politics of Baraka's time.

S O S includes all of the poems that appeared in *Transbluesency: The Selected Poems of LeRoi Jones/Amiri Baraka (1961–1995)*, as well as those in *Funk Lore: New Poems (1984–1995)*. The last section of this volume, "Fashion This," offers a sample of Baraka's poems from the period following, for the most part unpublished in book form. Although the first two collections were edited with Baraka's consultation and final approval, I regret that the last part of this book was compiled after the poet's death.

Throughout his life, as he transformed himself from "Beat" to Nationalist to Third World Socialist, Baraka remained a difficult figure to approach, particularly for a literary establishment positioned somewhere between Anglo-American academicism and the entertainment industry. As the noted anthologist M. L. Rosenthal wrote more than forty years ago, "No American poet since Pound has come closer to making poetry and politics reciprocal forms of action."* At least a decade earlier, in his 1960 anthology *The New Poets: American*

---

* *Salmagundi*, nos. 22–23 (1973), quoted in *The LeRoi Jones/Amiri Baraka Reader* (New York: Basic Books, 1999), xxi.

and British Poetry Since World War II, Rosenthal had praised the young, ostensibly "Beat" poet as possessing a "natural gift for quick, vivid imagery and spontaneous humor."* For a critic like Rosenthal, grounded in the Cold War university aestheticism of the fifties, the Beats' apolitical nonconformity, keeping rebellion and art "above" politics, wouldn't necessarily be a threat or a challenge. In the long run, such bohemianism wouldn't prove unfriendly—perhaps rather accommodating—to the legends of established institutions. However, an increasingly politicized avant-garde like Baraka's, committed to alternative forms of aesthetic and social behavior, was and *is* clearly another matter.

What distinguished him from the start is a kind of lyrical realism that sounds in counterpoint to his Beat contemporaries, steeped as they were in the egocentric idealism of nineteenth-century Anglo-American literature. Like Jack Spicer or Gilbert Sorrentino, *around* but not *of* the Beat public relations machinery, Baraka acknowledged a clear debt to the modernism of Pound and William Carlos Williams, while developing other more challenging measures throughout his career. It was, in essence, the experimental, materialist, and antiromantic overtones of the historical avant-gardes, as they filtered through Pound and Williams, that placed Baraka's writing in a new international tradition, both American (i.e., African American, of the "New World") and firmly outside Anglo-American culture.

In 1912 (the year F. T. Marinetti, flying 650 feet above the chimneys of Milan, heard the propeller declare the death of

* Ibid., xix.

the psychological self and the birth of a lyrical obsession with matter), Ezra Pound wrote that he, analogously, was in search of a more precise, active speech, "a language to think in."* Fifty years later, after two world wars, and with imperial America relentlessly on the march, Baraka's first book, *Preface to a Twenty Volume Suicide Note,* underlined the urgency of a comprehensive African-American poetic language. An early indication of this language's parameters may be found in "Hymn for Lanie Poo," fixing the historical ironies of the rebellious, colonial Rimbaud with the poem's epigraph: "*Vous êtes des faux Négres.*" The "Hymn" finds its pulse in a parodic reliquary of the avant-garde "Saint"—who, in a notorious letter to his high school literature teacher (having run off to Paris at age sixteen), clamored about the primal, "universal poetry" of mind and soul.** Baraka's young minstrel/bard ("*schwartze bohemian*" as he referred to himself and friends) opens this mock ode to the primordial with self-conscious slapstick, playing both inside and outside the subject at hand:

> O,
> these wild trees
> will make charming wicker baskets,
> the young woman
> the young black woman
> the young black beautiful woman
> said.

* Marinetti's "Technical Manifesto of Futurist Literature," from *Let's Murder the Moonshine: Selected Writings* (Los Angeles: Sun & Moon Press, 1991), 92; Pound's "A Retrospect," from *Literary Essays* (New York: New Directions, 1968), 3–4.
** Rimbaud, *Complete Works,* Wallace Fowlie ed. and trans. (University of Chicago Press), 1966, 304.

These wild-assed trees
will make charming
wicker baskets.

(now, I'm putting word in her mouth . . . tch).

In "Way Out West" (after Sonny Rollins's title composition on
the 1957 LP, and dedicated to Gary Snyder),* Baraka improvised
upon and reevaluated the rhetorical powers of that other grand
Anglo-American figure, T.S. Eliot. In the seeming infinitude of
Far Western space, the eyes of Prufrock's dream melody are made
to open wide, and to be shut with some finality at song's end:

No use for beauty
collapsed, with moldy breath
done in. Insidious weight
of cankered dreams. Tiresias'
weathered cock.

Walking into the sea, shells
caught in the hair. Coarse
waves tearing the tongue.

Closing the eyes. As
simple an act. You float

Further along, in the collage piece "Vice," he even more self-
consciously defined a topography he is struggling to inhabit.
He introduced the theme of rage in exile, from a language and
a culture, where the poem seems an incessant reminder of a
distance still to be traveled, a music still to be transformed:

* Recorded at the Contemporary Records studio in Los Angeles, March 7, 1957.

This is *not* rage. (I am not that beautiful!) Only
    immobile coughs & gestures
towards something I don't understand. If I were lucky
    enough to still be an
adolescent, I'd just attribute these weird singings in
    my intestine to sex, &
slink off merrily to masturbate. Mosaic of disorder I
    own but cannot recognize.
Mist in me.

In the sparsely lyrical and intimate "Betancourt" (dated, in the 'foreign' manner, "30 July 1960/Habana": marking Baraka's pivotal visit to Cuba), the exiled rage of "Vice" was momentarily reversed. He didn't look out at the world from inside the poem's U.S. boundaries, but rather from "some/ new greenness," surrounded by a bolder, more active language, where "flame/is the mind/ . . . on strange islands of warmth." In this exquisite instance he gazed at his land from outside, from a revolutionary island and distance, toward poem and country:

    (I mean I think
I know now
what a poem
is) A
turning away . . .
from what
it was
had moved
us . . .
       A
madness.

Back home, at the end of *Preface to a Twenty Volume Suicide Note*, the exile was once again complete: "Notes for a Speech" beginning "African blues / does not know me. Their steps, in sands/of their own/land. A country/in black & white, newspapers/blown down pavements . . . ," concluded with the inescapably reductive and terrible "democratic vista" of lower-case nationality:

> They shy away. My own
> dead souls, my, so called
> people. Africa
> is a foreign place. You are
> as any other sad man here
> american.

Baraka's first book underscores how the scrutiny of poetic language compelled him to redefine the ideological stance of the poet. Some ten years later, after his Nationalist phase, this research will ultimately bring him to a kind Internationalism, a Third World Socialist aesthetic of liberation. Up through his last poems, there remained above all a critical, often restless lyricism insisting that, to borrow a phrase from his *Blues People*, the piece must "swing—from verb to noun."

*   *   *

His second book, *The Dead Lecturer*, was published in 1964—the year *Dutchman* premiered and won an Obie, and not long before he moved from Greenwich Village to Harlem, and began his Nationalist phase. In several poems at the start of the collection, the lyric was turned on itself, or rather on the privileged figure of the poet ("Roi," as he signed himself until 1966).* With "Balboa, the Entertainer," Baraka pushed a musical intensity, a clarity of diction and phrasing, that's nothing short of disarming:

* Baraka was born Everett LeRoy Jones, changing his name to LeRoi in the fifties.

                    (The philosophers
of need, of which
I am lately
one,
        will tell you. "The People,"
(and not think themselves
liable
to the same
trembling flesh). I say now, "The People
as some lesson repeated, now,
the lights are off, to myself,
as a lover, or at the cold wind.

The next piece, "A Contract. (For the Destruction and
Rebuilding of Paterson," revisited the populist language of
W.C. Williams' civic icon (also Baraka's not-so-idyllic home
state), in order to demolish it from within. The poet found
it critical to attack "Paterson's" imaginative and mythopoetic
core, in rebuilding a secular, more democratic and demytholo-
gized city—and by extension, poetry—for those who must live
within its limits:

Flesh, and cars, tar, dug holes beneath stone
a rude hierarchy of money, band saws cross out
music, feeling. Even speech, corrodes.
                                    I came here
from where I sat boiling in my veins, cold fear
at the death of men, the death of learning, in
cold fear, at my own. Romantic vests of same death
blank at the corner, blank when they raise their fingers

Cross the hearts, in dark flesh staggered so marvelous
are their lies.

The rest of *The Dead Lecturer* resounded with a multiplicity of rhythms and dictions that by decade's end would make Baraka a preeminent voice in American poetry. Accents and poetic stances, subject matter and ideological reflections were in the foreground, as the poet seemed intent on challenging Cold War orthodoxies. Along with contemporaries outside the United States, he continued to work from the assumptions of a highly politicized avant-garde. The ideological lucidity, which defined the European and Third World poetics of the 1960s, claimed the urge of poetry to establish itself as the "conscience of communication."* The poem was conceived as a total, linguistic act, uniquely capable of posing the problem of language: a work critical of—and invaded by—mass media and governmental institutions, while remaining a primary symptom of reality. "The Politics of Rich Painters," for instance, displayed an articulate line, driven by the nuances of shifting, heterogeneous cadences, often spoken, often collaged, and always relentlessly material and public. This compositional mode would characterize his writing throughout the rest of the decade:

> Just their fingers' prints
> staining the cold glass, is sufficient
> for commerce, and a proper ruling on
> humanity. You know the pity
> of democracy, that we must sit here
> and listen to how he made his money.
> Tho the catalogue of his possible ignorance
> roars and extends through the room
> like fire. "Love," becomes the pass,
> the word taken intimately to combat
> all the uses of language. So that learning
> itself falls into disrepute.

* Adriano Spatola, "A Vaguely Ontological Aspiration," *Invisible City*, 16–17 (June 1975), 33; translated & reprinted from *TamTam*, 2 (Parma, 1972).

* * *

The leap from *The Dead Lecturer* to *Black Magic* in 1969—the quint-
essential volume of his Nationalist period and one of the most
influential publications of the Black Arts movement—doesn't
seem as extreme as many in the literary establishment, then and
now, would claim. The ideological urgency of earlier poems, such
as "A Guerrilla Handbook," can hardly be dismissed as bohemian:

            Silent political rain
    against the speech
    of friends. (we love them
    trapped in life, knowing no way out
    except description. Or black soil
    floating in the arm.
                        We must convince the living
                        that the dead
                        cannot sing.

The impetus of self-critical pieces in the first two sections of
Black Magic, like "Sabotage" and "Target Study," appears not so
different from the driving, hard-bop cadences of "Green Lan-
tern's Solo" in *The Dead Lecturer*.

    No, Nigger, no, blind drunk in SantaSurreal's
        beard. Dead hero
    for our time who would advance the nation's economy
        by poking holes
    in his arms. As golden arms build a forest of loves, and
        find only
    the heavy belly breath of ladies whispering their false
        pregnancies through the
    phone.

The awareness that urged his recasting of the rhetorical figure of the poet, which he had set in motion in the earlier collection, bore fruit in the clarity of many compositions in *Black Magic*, such as "Letter to E. Franklin Frazier":

> Those days I rose through the smoke of chilling
>   Saturdays
> hiding my eyes from the shine boys, my mouth and
>   my flesh
> from their sisters. I walked quietly and always
>   alone
> watching the cheap city like I thought it would swell
> and explode, and only my crooked breath could put it
>   together again.

The same may be said of the reflective energy that concludes "The People Burning." The poet's scrutiny not only embraces the poem, but undermines the very self-consciousness of the poetic act, emphasizing the difficulty of building poetry upon what Walter Benjamin calls "individual renunciation":*

> Sit down and forget it. Lean on your silence,
>   breathing
> the dark. Forget your whole life, pop your fingers in
>   a closed room,
> hopped-up witch doctor for the cowards of a recent
>   generation. It is
> choice, now, like a philosophy problem. It is choice,
>   now, and

* "To build a production on the basic renunciation of all manifest experiences of this class causes specific and considerable difficulties. These difficulties turn this poetry into an esoteric poetry." From "Addendum to 'The Paris of the Second Empire of Baudelaire,'" *Invisible City*, 21–22 (November 1977), 33.

the weight is specific and personal. It is not an
emotional decision.

There are facts, and who was it said, that this is a
scientific century.

How Baraka described his former nationalist politics in 1973–
74—as he helped transform the Congress of Afrikan Peoples into a
Marxist-Leninist organization—could also account for his politics
from that moment through to his later years. Publicly altering
what he characterized as his "narrow nationalist and bourgeois
nationalist stand," and repudiating it as, in fact, "reactionary,"* he
went on to point out that his intentions as a Third World Socialist
were fundamentally like those he held as a Nationalist:

> They were similar in the sense I see art as a weapon
> of revolution. It's just that I define revolution
> in Marxist terms. I once defined revolution in
> Nationalist terms. But I came to my Marxist view
> as a result of having struggled as a Nationalist
> and found certain dead ends theoretically and
> ideologically, as far as Nationalism was concerned
> and had to reach out for a communist ideology. **

With this declaration of Marxist-Leninism, a curious thing hap-
pened to his publishing career. Starting with the mimeo edition
of the groundbreaking *Hard Facts, 1973–1975*, which formally
signaled this ideological shift, down through the two aforemen-
tioned collections, *Transbluescency* (1995) and *Funk Lore* (1996),
he would only be published by smaller or alternative presses. In
the poet's own words, from an interview in 1996: "When I was

* KPFK, Los Angeles radio interview, March 1976; transcribed in part in
Invisible City, 23–25 (March 1979), 8.
** *The Amiri Baraka/LeRoi Jones Reader*, xxviii.

saying, 'White people go to hell,' I never had trouble finding a publisher. But when I was saying, 'Black and white, unite and fight, destroy capitalism,' then you suddenly get to be unreasonable."*

After breaking with cultural nationalism, Baraka soon emerged as an artist in the radical tradition of Cesar Vallejo, Luis Aragon, Paul Éluard, Aimé Césaire, and René Depestre. Insisting that poetry be an active, sociolinguistic force, Baraka would pursue a utopian communist aesthetic, much like what Aragon and Éluard called "lyrical communism." Invariably the poet would seek allegiance between what is radical or subversive politically and what is avant-garde poetically.

Moreover, as an African-American poet, Baraka's career embodied a commitment, along with poets like Césaire and Depestre, to develop a space for the spirit of negritude within this internationalism. For him, negritude played at the heart of twentieth-century poetics, animating and transforming what remained innovative in the socialist literary project. As Depestre noted, "The new Black Orpheus will be a revolutionary or he will be nothing at all."**

Many have emphasized in Baraka's work the exemplars of progressive, as well as traditional jazz and blues. It afforded a model for a genuinely avant-idiom, inspired by Third World and European art practices alike, to fashion its own singular, African-American poetics. In this respect, Baraka described what, at the close of a century, he considered fresh and contemporary; the language and music that reality spoke through him:

If you're a modern artist who's not some kind of cultural nationalist, you understand that you can learn from anything and anybody, see that the whole of world culture is at your

* Obituary, *Los Angeles Times*, January 10, 2014.
** Speech to the 1967 Tricontinental Cultural Congress in Havana, reprinted in *Invisible City*, 10 (October 1973), 9.

disposal, because no one people has created the monuments of art and culture in the world, it's been collective.*

*　*　*

The poet's later work shows music and history to be for him inevitable subjects of poetry. From the terse, hard-swinging lines of poems like "Four Cats on REPATRIATIONOLOGY":

> Dude asked Monk
> If he was interested
>
> In digging
> The Mother
> Land
>
> Monk say,
> "I was in the
> Motherfuckin
> Mother Land
> before
>
> & some mother
> fucka
>
> brought me
> over here
>
> to play
> the
> mother
> fuckin

---

* KGNU, Boulder, Colorado, broadcast, July 27, 1984; transcribed in part in the *Amiri Baraka/LeRoi Jones Reader*, 249–50.

piano. . . .

You, dig?"

And from the longer, more fluid, almost ballad-like measures of "Chamber Music," with their poignant introspection:

> I am like that sometimes, I think, some distant romantic wrapped in music. I wanted to know myself, and found that was a lifetime's work, the twists and zig zags, dips and turns, all could disorient you, that you were no longer you but somebody else masquerading as yourself 's desire. Rain could come. The sky grow light. It could even be twilight, in a foreign town. Where you walked under far noises of invisible worlds.

Baraka's lyrical gift remained always *of* and *for* the world, and the people's music that daily inspired it.

His powers can't be said to have diminished; if anything, their resonance matured and deepened in this final section. Baraka was never just an imitator of blues or jazz idioms, but strove to grow with the music, to develop a language that embraced and played along with it, if you will. More than a singer, he was a vital composer and improviser in the historical ensemble. Always ready to swing and be "truthful as the actual life of the world."

The poem, "Fashion This, from the Irony of the World," begins with up-tempo comedic rhythms, the poet as much amused and bemused with himself as with his audience:

> That I, the undaunted Laureate of the place, daunted in some

Un as yet/ed pre tense of what they see, they be
As if, such where they was
Was yet to be, and then to say
They is, and is not, like revelations, wow!
Humans. The skin. The lodging inside dumbness a
slight breeze frees they speech
To speak as if acquainted with small things in the
world. Eating, Belching, Farting,
Murder, Robbery.
And so. As if, and them too they is. But nothing
further
But the wee dots on the deletion resembling the minds
of them
Yet to come.

Masterful turn after masterful turn, Baraka drives the stakes higher, pushing one to feel the sounds of an increasingly discomforting, ridiculous, and monstrous world. Indeed, one is compelled to end with the overwhelming question, "what next the world of this life held for / those / Who would love goodness."

The musicality of Baraka's earlier books is challenged and extended to where it's inseparable from his thinking. It would reveal, as he wrote in his eulogy of Miles Davis, "a prayer in the future."* Song and thought were in close harmony, and there was an ease of rhythm and accent that embodied his late mastery. Poems may have served what, for Baraka, became an international struggle, while his technique, full of humor and no less extraordinary as it became abbreviated with age, would remain a "test of the poet's sincerity," once more to quote Pound.**

* "When Miles Split," *Eulogies* (New York: Marsilio, 1996), 144.
** *ABC of Reading* (New York: New Directions, 1960), 203.

In a more recent piece from 2009, "All Songs Are Crazy," the poet is joyous to the challenge:

> I who have learned singing from the oldest singers
> In the world and have sung some songs myself
> Want to create that song that everybody knows
> And that everybody will sing one day.
> So what is left to do? That is how the song
> Begins.

Here, alongside the last two lines in Baraka's typescript, there's a long-hand notation in parenthesis, to serve as a performance cue, as well as, one can't help but imagine, a nod to posterity: *(sing)*.

—Paul Vangelisti
Los Angeles, May 1, 2014

PREFACE TO A TWENTY VOLUME SUICIDE NOTE

1961

Preface to a Twenty Volume Suicide Note

for Kellie Jones, born 16 May 1959

Lately, I've become accustomed to the way
The ground opens up and envelopes me
Each time I go out to walk the dog.
Or the broad edged silly music the wind
Makes when I run for a bus . . .

Things have come to that.

And now, each night I count the stars,
And each night I get the same number.
And when they will not come to be counted,
I count the holes they leave.

Nobody sings anymore.

And then last night, I tiptoed up
To my daughter's room and heard her
Talking to someone, and when I opened
The door, there was no one there . . .
Only she on her knees, peeking into

Her own clasped hands.

March 1957

Hymn for Lanie Poo

Vous êtes des faux Nègres
—*Rimbaud*

O,
these wild trees
will make charming wicker baskets,
the young woman
the young black woman
the young black beautiful woman
said.

>   These wild-assed trees
>   will make charming
>   wicker baskets.

(now, I'm putting words in her mouth . . . tch)

1

All afternoon
we watched the cranes
humping each other

>   dropped
>   our shadows
>   onto the beach

and covered them over with sand.

Beware the evil sun . . .
turn you black

4

turn your hair

crawl your eyeballs

rot your teeth.

All afternoon
we sit around
near the edge of the city
                              hacking open
                              crocodile skulls
                              sharpening our teeth.
The god I pray to
got black boobies
got steatopygia

make faces in the moon
make me a greenpurple &
maroon winding sheet.
                              I wobble out to
                              the edge of the water

give my horny yell
& 24 elephants
stomp out of the subway
with consecrated hardons.

(watch out for that evil sun
turn you black)
                    My fireface

my orange
and fireface
squat by the flames.

She had her coming out party
with 3000 guests
from all parts of the country.
Queens, Richmond, Togoland, The Camerooons;
A white hunter, very unkempt,
with long hair,
whizzed in on the end of a vine.
(spoke perfect english too.)

"Throw on another goddamned Phoenecian,"
I yelled, really getting with it.

John Coltrane arrived with an Egyptian lady.
he played very well.

"Throw on another goddamned Phoenecian."

We got so drunk (Hulan Jack
brought his bottle of Thunderbird),
nobody went hunting
the next morning.

   2

o,
don't be shy honey.
we all know
these wicker baskets
would make wild-assed trees.

Monday, I spent most of the day hunting
Knocked off about six, gulped down a cou-

ple of monkey foreskins, then took in a
flick. Got to bed early.

Tuesday, same thing all day. (Caught a
mangy lioness with one tit.) Ate.
Watched television for awhile. Read the
paper, then hit the sack.

Wednesday, took the day off.
Took the wife and kids to the games.
Read Garmanda's book, "14 Tribes of
Ambiguity," didn't like it.

Thursday, we caught a goddamn ape.
Must've weighed about 600 pounds.
We'll probably eat ape meat for the
rest of the month. Christ, I hate
ape meat.

Friday, I stayed home with a supposed
cold. Goofed the whole day trying to
rethatch the roof. Had run in with
the landlord.

We spent the weekend at home.
I tried to get some sculpting done,
but nothing came of it. It's impos-
sible to be an artist and a bread
winner at the same time.
Sometimes I think I oughta chuck
the whole business.

3

The firemasons parade.

(The sun is using this country
as a commode.

Beware the sun, my love.)

The firemasons are very square.
They are supposed to be a civic
and fraternal organization, but
all they do is have parades and
stay high. They also wear funny
looking black hats, which are
round and have brims. The fire-
masons are cornballs.

4

Each morning
I go down
to Gansevoort St.
and stand on the docks.
I stare out
at the horizon
until it gets up
and comes to embrace
me. I
make believe
it is my father.
This is known
as genealogy.

5

We came into the
silly little church
shaking our wet raincoats
on the floor.
It wasn't water,
that made the raincoats
wet.
  The preacher's
  conning eyes
  filed when he saw
  the way I walked to-
  wards him; almost
  throwing my hips out
  of whack.
  He screamed,

He's wet with the blood of the lamb!!

And everybody
got real happy.

 6 (die schwartze Bohemien)

They laught,

and religion was something

he fount in coffee ships, by God.

It's not that I got enything
against cotton, nosiree, by God

It's just that . . .

                Man lookatthatblonde

                          whewee!

I think they are not treating us like

Mr. Lincun said they should

                    or Mr. Gandhi

For that matter. By God.

        ZEN

is a bitch! Like "Bird" was,

                Cafe Olay

for me, Miss.

             But white cats can't swing . . .

Or the way this guy kept patronizing me—

like he was Bach or somebody

                   Oh, I knew

John Kasper when he hung around with shades . . .

                      She's a painter, Man.

It's just that it's such a drag to go
Way uptown for Bar B Cue,
                By God . . .

How much?

About my sister.

> (O, generation revered
> above all others.
> O, generation of fictitious
> Ofays
>> I revere you . . .
>> You are all so beautiful)

my sister drives a green jaguar
my sister has her hair done twice a month
my sister is a school teacher
my sister took ballet lessons
my sister has a fine figure: never diets
my sister doesn't like to teach in Newark
   because there are too many colored
   in her classes
my sister hates loud shades
my sister's boy friend is a faggot music teacher
   who digs Tschaikovsky
my sister digs Tschaikovsky also
it is because of this similarity of interests
that they will probably get married.

> Smiling & glad/in
> the huge & loveless
> white-anglo sun/of
> benevolent step
> mother America.

In Memory of Radio

Who has ever stopped to think of the divinity of Lamont
    Cranston?
(Only Jack Kerouac, that I know of: & me.
The rest of you probably had on WCBS and Kate Smith,
Or something equally unattractive.)

What can I say?
It is better to have loved and lost
Than to put linoleum in your living rooms?

Am I a sage or something?
Mandrake's hypnotic gesture of the week?
(Remember, I do not have the healing powers of Oral Roberts . . .
I cannot, like F. J. Sheen, tell you how to get saved & *rich!*
I cannot even order you to gaschamber satori like Hitler or
    Goody Knight

& Love is an evil word.
Turn it backwards/see, see what I mean?
An evol word. & besides
who understands it?
I certainly wouldn't like to go out on that kind of limb.

Saturday mornings we listened to *Red Lantern* & his undersea folk.
At 11, *Let's Pretend/&* we did/& I, the poet, still do, Thank God!

What was it he used to say (after the transformation, when he was safe
& invisible & the unbelievers couldn't throw stones?) "Heh, heh, heh,
Who knows what evil lurks in the hearts of men? The Shadow knows."

O, yes he does
O, yes he does.
An evil word it is,
This Love.

Look for You Yesterday, Here You Come Today

Part of my charm:
        envious blues feeling
        separation of church & state
        grim calls from drunk debutantes

Morning never aids me in my quest.
I have to trim my beard in solitude.
I try to hum lines from "The Poet In New York".

People saw metal all around the house on Saturdays. The
        Phone rings.

terrible poems come in the mail. Descriptions of celibate parties
        torn trousers: Great Poets dying
        with their strophes on. & me
        incapable of a simple straightforward
        anger.

It's so diffuse
being alive. Suddenly one is aware
        that nobody really gives a damn.
        My wife is pregnant with *her* child.
        "It means nothing to me", sez Strindberg.

14

An avalanche of words
could cheer me up. Words from Great Sages.
                Was James Karolis a great sage??
                Why did I let Ora Matthews beat him up
                in the bathroom? Haven't I learned my lesson.

I would take up painting
If I cd think of a way to do it
better than Leonardo. Than Bosch
Than Hogarth. Than Kline.

Frank walked off the stage, singing
"My silence is as important as Jack's incessant yatter."

I am a mean hungry sorehead.
Do I have the capacity for grace??

To arise one smoking spring
& find one's youth has taken off
for greener parts.

A sudden blankness in the day
as if there were no afternoon.
& all my piddling joys retreated
to their own dopey mythic worlds.

The hours of the atmosphere
grind their teeth like hags.

                    (When will world war two be over?)

I stood up on a mailbox
waving my yellow tee-shirt

watching the grey tanks
stream up Central Ave.

> All these thots
> are Flowers Of Evil
> cold & lifeless
> as subway rails

the sun like a huge cobblestone
flaking its brown slow rays
primititi

> once, twice, . My life
> seems over & done with.
> Each morning I rise
> like a sleep walker
> & rot a little more.

All the lovely things I've known have disappeared.
I have all my pubic hair & am lonely.
There is probably no such place as BattleCreek, Michigan!

Tom Mix dead in a Boston Nightclub
before I realized what happened.

People laugh when I tell them about Dickie Dare!
What is one to do in an alien planet
where the people breath New Ports?
Where is my space helmet, I sent for it
3 lives ago . . . when there were box tops.

What has happened to box tops??

O, God . . . I must have a belt that glows green
in the dark. Where is my Captain Midnight decoder??
I can't understand what Superman is saying!

THERE *MUST* BE A LONE RANGER!!!

****

but this also
is part of my charm.
A maudlin nostalgia
that comes on
like terrible thoughts about death.

How dumb to be sentimental about anything
To call it love
& cry pathetically
into the long black handkerchief
of the years.

> "Look for you yesterday
> Here you come today
> Your mouth wide open
> But what you got to say?"

> —part of my charm

> old envious   blues feeling
> ticking like   a big cobblestone clock.

I hear the reel running out . . .
the spectators are impatient for popcorn:
It was only a selected short subject

F. Scott Charon
will soon be glad-handing me
like a legionaire

My silver bullets all gone
My black mask trampled in the dust

& Tonto way off in the hills
moaning like Bessie Smith.

To a Publisher . . . Cut-out

The blight rests in your face.
For your unknown musiks. The care & trust
Undeliberate. Like an axe-murder
Or flat pancake. The night cold & asexual
A long sterile moon lapping at the dank Hudson.
The end of a star. The water more than any
Other thing. We are dibbled here. Seurat's
Madness. That kind of joke. Isolate
Land creatures in a wet unfriendly world.

We must be strong. (smoke Balkan Sobranie)
People will think you have the taste
In this hyar family. Some will stroke your face.
Better posture is another thing. Watch out for Peanuts,
he's gonna turn out bad/ A J.D./ A Beatnik! A
Typical wise-ass N.Y. kid. "X" wanted to bet me
that Charlie Brown spent most of his time
whacking his doodle, or having weird relations
with that dopey hound of his (though that's
a definite improvement over "Arf Arf" & that
filthy little lesbian hes hung up with.)

As if any care could see us through. Could defend us.
Save us from you, Little Darling. Or me, which is worse.

"A far far worser thing I do/than I has ever done".
Put that in your pipe & watch out for the gendarmes.
They arresses people for less than that. For less
Than we are ever capable of. Any kind of sincerity

    Guarantees complete disregard. Complete abnegation.
    "Must dig with my fingers/as nobody will lend me
    or sell me a pick axe." Axe the man who owns one.
    Hellzapoppin. The stars might not come on tonight . . .
    & who the hell can do anything about that?? Eh,
    Milord/ Milady/ The kind Dubarry wasn't. Tres slick.

But who am I to love anybody? I ride the 14th St. bus
every day . . . reading Hui neng/ Raymond Chandler! Olson . . .
I have slept with almost every mediocre colored woman
On 23rd St . . . At any rate, talked a good match. And
Frightened by the lack of any real communication
I addressed several perfumed notes to Uncle Don
& stuffed them into the radio. In the notes,
Of course, crude assignations, off color suggestions,
Diagrams of new methods for pederasts, lewd poems
That rime. IF ONLY HE WOULD READ THESE ON THE AIR.
(There are other things could take my mind from
this childe's play . . . but none nearly as interesting.)

I long to be a mountain climber
& wave my hands up 8,000 feet.
Out of sight & snow blind/the tattered
Stars and Stripes poked in the new peak.

& come down later, Clipper by my side,
To new wealth & eternal fame. That
Kind of care. I could wear

Green corduroy coats & felt tyroleans
For the rest of my days; & belong to clubs.

Grandeur in boldness. Big & stupid as the wind.
But so lovely. Who's to understand that kind of con?
As if each day, after breakfast, someone asked you,
"What do you want to be when you grow up??" &
Day in, Day out, you just kept belching.

OSTRICHES & GRANDMOTHERS!

All meet here with us, finally: the
uptown, way-west, den of inconstant
moralities.
Faces up: all
my faces turned up
to the sun.

1

Summer's mist nods against the trees
till distance grows in my head
like an antique armada
dangled motionless from the horizon.

Unbelievable changes. Restorations.
Each day like my niña's fan
tweaking the flat air
back and forth till the room
is a blur of flowers.

Intimacy takes on human form . . .
& sheds it like a hide.
                           Lips, eyes,
tiny lace coughs
reflected on night's stealth.

2

Tonight, one star.
eye of the dragon.
                    The Void
signaling.
Reminding someone
it's still there.

3

It's these empty seconds
I fill with myself. Each
a recognition. A complete
utterance.

Here, it is color; motion;
the feeling of dazzling beauty
Flight.

As
the trapeze rider
leans
with arms spread

wondering at the bar's
delay

SCENARIO VI

. . . and I come out of it
with this marvelous yellow cane
in my hand, yellow cashmere jacket
green felt pants & green boater . . . & green &
black clack shoes, polished & fast, jiggling
in the wings . . . till Vincente says "rollllem"
& I jiggle out on the stage, hands in my pockets,
the cane balanced delicately under my arm, spinning
& clack clack clacking across the bare sunday clothesline
tilting the hat to avoid the sun & ginergerly missing
the dried branch I had put there yesterday.

The motion of the mind! Smooooth; I jiggle
& clack stomping one foot & the clothesline swings.
Fabulei Verwachsenes. Ripping this one off
in a series of dramatic half-turns I learned
many years ago in the orient; Baluba:
"The power to cloud men's minds" &c., which
I'm sure you must have heard about, doodle-doo.
& then I'm sitting in this red chair, humming,
feet still pecking at the marble floor, the
line motionless with only the tiniest leaf
on the dead branch waving, slowly, with a red background,

& I can't see anything, only hear this raspy 1936 voice
singing in german a very groovy love song; to me.

There's a train whistle, too. In and out like this.
When out the open window of early spring, sharp
browns & greens fuzzy through the shade
& a fence somehow too bleak to describe, or even
be made sad by.

& I'm not even breathing hard. Tapping my feet
so nicely, the cane too, on the red marble. No
echo, that's distant thunder for these early summer storms,
cools off the whole scene too. But waiting
for my next cue, Vincente comes over, lights my cigarette,
We make a date for next wednesday, at the rainbow hut,
& he has a fabulous cigarette holder. & he pats
my cane-hand & says, "you do it up, baby". I'm on again.

Sylvia has come out in her smashing oranges & jewelry,
she has her mouth wide & I can hear her listening to
my feet clackings for her deep beauty doesn't include
rhythm. But we make it in great swirls out to the terrace,
which overlooks Sumer . . . & the Indus river, where next
week probably all kinds of white trash will ride in
on stolen animals we will be amazed by.

Way Out West

for Gary Snyder

As simple an act
as opening the eyes. Merely
coming into things by degrees.

Morning: some tear is broken
on the wooden stairs
of my lady's eyes. Profusions
of green. The leaves. Their
constant prehensions. Like old
junkies on Sheridan Square, eyes
cold and round. There is a song
Nat Cole sings . . . This city
& the intricate disorder
of the seasons.

Unable to mention
something as abstract as time.

Even so, (bowing low in thick
smoke from cheap incense; all
kinds questions filling the mouth,
till you suffocate & fall dead
to opulent carpet.) Even so,

shadows will creep over your flesh
& hide your disorder, your lies.

There are unattractive wild ferns
outside the window
where the cats hide. They yowl
from there at nights. In heat
& bleeding on my tulips.

Steel bells, like the evil
unwashed Sphinx, towing in the twilight.
Childless old murderers, for centuries
with musty eyes.

I am distressed. Thinking
of the seasons, how they pass,
how I pass, my very youth, the
ripe sweet of my life; drained off . . .

Like giant rhesus monkeys;
picking their skulls,
with ingenious cruelty
sucking out the brains.

No use for beauty
collapsed, with moldy breath
done in. Insidious weight
of cankered dreams. Tiresias'
weathered cock.

Walking into the sea, shells
caught in the hair. Coarse
waves tearing the tongue.

Closing the eyes. As
simple an act. You float

THE BRIDGE

for wieners & mcclure

I have forgotten the head
of where I am. Here at the bridge. 2
bars, down the street, seeming
to wrap themselves around my fingers, the day,
screams in me; pitiful like a little girl
you sense will be dead before the winter
is over.

I can't see the bridge now, I've past
it, its shadow, we drove through, headed out
along the cold insensitive roads to what
we wanted to call "ourselves."
"How does the bridge go?" Even tho
you find yourself in its length
strung out along its breadth, waiting
for the cold sun to tear out your eyes. Enamoured
of its blues, spread out in the silk clubs of
this autumn tune. The changes are difficult, when
you hear them, & know they are all in you, the chords

of your disorder meddle with your would be disguises.
Sifting in, down, upon your head, with the sun & the insects.

(Late feeling) Way down till it barely, after that rush of
wind & odor reflected from hills you have forgotten the color
when you touch the water, & it closes, slowly, around your head.
The bridge will be behind you, that music you know, that place,
you feel when you look up to say, it is me, & I have forgotten,
all the things, you told me to love, to try to understand, the
bridge will stand, high up in the clouds & the light, & you,

(when you have let the song run out) will be sliding through
unmentionable black.

VICE

Sometimes I feel I have to express myself
and then, whatever it is I have to express
falls out of my mouth like flakes of ash
from a match book that the drunken guest
at the grey haired jew lady's birthday party has
set on fire, for fun & to ease the horrible boredom.

& when these flakes amass, I make serious collages
or empty them (feinting a gratuitous act) out the window
on the heads of the uncurious puerto rican passersby.

ACT I. The celibate bandit pees in the punch bowl.

(curious image) occurring friday evening, a house
full of middle class women & a photogenic baker.
Baby bear has eaten her porridge, had her bath, shit
& gone to sleep. Smoke rises (strange for mid-summer)
out of a strange little shack in the middle of the
torn down cathedral. Everything seems to be light green.
I suppose, a color of despair or wretchedness. Anyway,
everything is light green, even the curling little hairs
on the back of my hand, and the old dog scar glinting
in the crooked (green, light green) rays of an unshaded bulb.

There doesn't seem to be any act 2. The process is stopped.
Functional, as a whip, a strong limb broken off in the gale
lying twisty & rotten, unnoticed in my stone back yard.
All this means nothing is happening to me (in this world).
I suppose some people are having a ball. Organized fun.
Pot Smokers Institute is going on an outing tomorrow; my
corny sister, in her fake bohemian pants, is borrowing something
else. (A prestige item). These incomprehensible dullards!

Asked to be special, & alive in the mornings, if they are green
& I am still alive, (& green) hovering above all the things I
seem to want to be a part of (curious smells, the high-noon idea
of life . . . a crowded train station where they broadcast a slice,
just one green slice, of some glamourous person's life).
& I cant even isolate my pleasures. All the things I can talk about
mean nothing to me.

This is *not* rage. (I am not that beautiful!) Only immobile coughs
& gestures towards somethings I don't understand. If I were lucky
enough to still be an adolescent, I'd just attribute these weird
singings in my intestine to sex, & slink off merrily to mastur
bate. Mosaic of disorder I own but cannot recognize. Mist in me.

There must be some great crash in the slinky world: MYSTIC
    CURE . . .
Cunning panacea of the mind. The faith of it. the singed hairs
of human trust, corrupt & physical as a disease. A glass stare.

Resolution, for the quick thrust of epee, to force your opponent
cringing against the wall, not in anger, but unfettered happiness
while your lady is watching from the vined balcony, your triumph.

& years after, you stand in subways watching your invincible hand
bring the metal to bear again & again, when you are old & the
 lady,
(o, fond memories we hide in our money belts, & will not spend)
the lady, you young bandits who have not yet stolen your first purse

the lady will be dead.

And if you are alone (if there is something in you so cruel)

You will wonder at the extravagance

of youth.

SYMPHONY SID

First
take the first
thing. Blue. The mountain,
largest of our
landscape. From
a dark hall at
the bottom, the shapes
a shadow, without
hardness, or that
ugly smell of
blackening flesh.
    The scale
is music, black shadow
from highest wild
fingers placing evening
beneath our
tongues.
   A man, a woman
shaking the night apart. Forget
who you are. Forget
my fingers.

BETANCOURT

for Rubi

What are
influences?
              A green truck
wet & glowing, seance
of ourselves, elegy for the sea
at night, my flesh
a woman's, at the fingertips
soft white increased coolness
from the dark
sea.
          We sat
with our backs
to the sea. Not
in the gardens
of Spain, but some
new greenness, birds
scorching the yellow
rocks at the foot
of the sea's wall. A barrier
of rock, tilting backwards, damp,
thrown up against
a floating dreary
disgust. Even fear
without that self possession. The

night's defection. Walking all night
entwined inside, I mean
I tasted you, your real & fleshy
voice
inside my head
& choked
as if some primitive
corruption re-sat
itself in full view
of a puritan flame. And flame
is the mind, the wet hands
mark on strange islands
of warmth.
                    Big stone nose, nigger
lips, the entire head
thrust from
a serpents snout. Idle
somehow, fire scorching
the plain earth we pulled
up around thinking
to limit its violence. To
contain even that
madness (within
some thrown wall
of words.)
                    Our gestures
are silence. The sea's
wet feathers slowly
black. (You die
from mornings, looking down
from that silence
at the silence
of roofs. Disconnected

flesh. Not even cars
from this distance
are real.

2

This
is slower. Infused (somehow)
with sound
& distance. Slow

the cock
flat
on skin
like
a dead
insect. A
bee, with
crushed
antlers,
sprawled
on its side,
        And last night, talking to ourselves, except
when some wildness
cut us, ripped impossibly
deep beneath black
flesh
to black bone. Then
we loved each other. Understood
the miles of dead air
between our
softest parts. French girl
from the desert. Desert man,

whose mind is some rotting
country of snow.

3

There is more
underneath. Rotted, green
beneath hands making
their deadly wishes
show. La casa. El edificio. La
Mar. El hombre. Without seething
tin braziers, no, those weird cups
in novels: chalices.
                         I was reading
some old man's poems
this morning. A lover
hid himself under
the stink of low trailing
sea birds, heavy sun, pure
distance. He had to go away,
I mean, from all of us, even
you, marvelous person
at the sea's edge. Even you
Sra. de Jiminez. Rubi.
                   And
I think he knew
all this would happen, that
when I dropped the book
the sky would have already
moved, turned black, and
wet grey air
would mark the windows.

                              That
there are fools
who hang close
to their original
thought. Elementals
of motion (Not, again,
that garden) but some
slightness
of feeling
they think is sweet
and long to die
inside.
                    Think
about it! As even
this, now, a turning
away. (I mean I think
I know now
what a poem
is) A
turning away . . .
from what
it was
had moved
us . . .
                    A
madness.
                    Looking at the sea. And some
white fast boat.

30 July 1960
Habana

THE INSIDIOUS DR. FU MAN CHU

If I think myself
strong, then I am
not true to the misery
in my life. The uncertainty.
(of what I am saying, who
I have chose to become, the
very air pressing my skin
held gently away, this woman
and the one I taste continually
in my nebular pallet tongue face
mouth feet, standing in piles
of numbers, hills, lovers.

                                        If
I think myself ugly
& go to the mirror, smiling,
at the inaccuracy, or now
the rain pounds dead grass
in the stone yard, I think
how very wise I am. How very
very wise.

THE NEW SHERIFF

There is something
in me so cruel, so
silent. It hesitates
to sit on the grass
with the young white
                    virgins
of my time. The blood-
letter, clothed in what
it is. Elemental essence,
animal grace, not that, but
a rude stink of color
huger, more vast, than
this city suffocating. Red
street. Waters noise
in the ear, inside
the hard bone
of the brain. Inside
the soft white meat
of the feelings. Inside
your flat white stomach
I move my tongue

From an Almanac

In the nature
of flesh, these clown gods
are words, blown
in the winters, thou
windows, lacking
sun.
          In the nature,
of ideas, in the nature of
words, these
clown god's are
winter. Are blown
thru our windows.
                    The flesh
& bone
of the season. Each
dead thing
hustled
across the pavement. Each
dead word
drowned
in a winter wind. Are
in the nature
of flesh. These
liars, clown
gods

FROM AN ALMANAC (2)

Respect the season
and dance to the rattle
of its bones.
                    The flesh
hung
from trees. Blown
down. A cold
music. A colder
hand, will grip
you. Your bare
soul. (Where is the soul's place. What is
its
nature?) Winter rattles
like the throat
of the hanged man. Swung
against our windows.
                    As bleak
as our thots. As wild
as that wind
we make (between
us).
            Can you dance? Shall
you?

From an Almanac (3)

for C.O.

This bizness, of dancing, how
can it suit us? Old men, naked
sterile women.
                    (our time,
a cruel one. Our soul's warmth
left out. Little match children,
dance
against the weather.
) The soul's
warmth
is how
shall I say
it,
        Its own. A place
of warmth, for children
wd dance there,
                    if they cd. If they
left their brittle selves behind (our time's
a cruel one.
                    Children
of winter. (I cross myself
like religion
                    Children
of a cruel time. (the wind

stirs the bones
& they drag clumsily
thru the cold.)
                    These children
are older
than their worlds. and
cannot dance.

NOTES FOR A SPEECH

African blues
does not know me. Their steps, in sands
of their own
land. A country
in black & white, newspapers
blown down pavements
of the world. Does
not feel
what I am.
   Strength
in the dream, an oblique
suckling of nerve, the wind
throws up sand, eyes
are something locked in
hate, of hate, of hate, to
walk abroad, they conduct
their deaths apart
from my own. Those
heads, I call
my "people."
   (And who are they. People. To concern
myself, ugly man. Who
you, to concern
the white flat stomachs

of maidens, inside houses
dying. Black. Peeled moon
light on my fingers
move under
her clothes. Where
is her husband. Black
words throw up sand
to eyes, fingers of
their private dead. Whose
soul, eyes, in sand. My color
is not theirs. Lighter, white man
talk. They shy away. My own
dead souls, my, so called
people. Africa
is a foreign place. You are
as any other sad man here
american.

THE DEAD LECTURER
1964

As a Possible Lover

Practices
silence, the way of wind
bursting
its early lull. Cold morning
to night, we go so
slowly, without
thought
to ourselves. (Enough
to have thought
tonight, nothing
finishes it. What
you are, will have
no certainty, or
end. That you will
stay, where you are,
a human gentle wisp
of life. Ah . . .)
                        practices
loneliness,
as a virtue. A single
specious need
to keep
what you have
never really
had.

BALBOA, THE ENTERTAINER

It cannot come
except you make it
from materials
it is not
caught from. (The philosophers
of need, of which
I am lately
one,
        will tell you. "The People,"
(and not think themselves
liable
to the same
trembling flesh). I say now, "The People,
as some lesson repeated, now,
the lights are off, to myself,
as a lover, or at the cold wind.

Let my poems be a graph
of me. (And they keep
to the line, where flesh
drops off. You will go
blank at the middle. A
dead man.

But
die soon, Love. If
what you have for
yourself, does not
stretch to your body's
end.
        (Where, without
preface,
music trails, or your fingers
slip
from my arm

A Contract. (For the Destruction and Rebuilding of Paterson

Flesh, and cars, tar, dug holes beneath stone
a rude hierarchy of money, band saws cross out
music, feeling. Even speech, corrodes.
                                            I came here
from where I sat boiling in my veins, cold fear
at the death of men, the death of learning, in
cold fear, at my own. Romantic vests of same death
blank at the corner, blank when they raise their fingers

Criss the hearts, in dark flesh staggered so marvelous
are their lies. So complete, their mastery, of these
stupid niggers. Loud spics kill each other, and will not

make the simple trip to Tiffany's. Will not smash their
    stainless
heads, against the simpler effrontery of so callous a code as gain.

You are no brothers, dirty woogies, dying under dried rinds,
    in massa's
droopy tuxedos. Cab Calloways of the soul, at the soul's juncture, a
music, they think will save them from our eyes. (In back of
    the terminal

where the circus will not go. At the backs of crowds, stooped
    and vulgar
breathing hate syllables, unintelligible rapes of all that linger in
our new world. Killed in white fedora hats, they stand so mute
    at what

whiter slaves did to my father. They muster silence. They pray
    at the
steps of abstract prisons, to be kings, when all is silence, when all
is stone. When even the stupid fruit of their loins is gold, or
    something
else they cannot eat.

THIS IS THE CLEARING I ONCE SPOKE OF

The talk scared him. Left alone, with me,
at some water. (Suddenness of your mind,
because you will be saved. Stand there
counting deaths. My own, is what I wanted
you to say, Roi, you will die soon.)

                             And
it went well, till evening, and the birds
fled. Their trees hanging empty at the
river. All of it a creation. More than
ideas. The simple elegant hand, a man
will extend. More than we can lose, and
still talk lovingly of "ourselves."

The brush sank behind its silence. This
was a jungle, dead children of thought.
We sat looking, and the wind changed
our fire, it was blue, and sang slowly.

Whose mind has this here? The way love
will move. I love you, I say that now
evenly, without emotion. Having
lost you. Or sitting, at the ruptured
threads of light. Wind and birds, spurn
out over the water, silent or dead.

A Poem for Neutrals

A japanese neon landscape blinks
a constant film
of memory. His leaves, his hills
change in dumb perspective. Farmers
and Americans,
                          say they are blue. Some natural phenomenon
some possible image
of what we shall call history. A jungle
of feeling. In their minds, the broken
tree, wet blood in the romantic's bulb. our sudden
and misconceived beauty. Inept tenderness. (For
those long girls lay in darkness under our smell.
Those talkers who will not shut up
when the dawn comes. And stand in doorways
letting cold air blow in.
                          It is a history of motive,
as secure as the economy
for these restless dwarfs
performing miracles for the blind. The wet ring
on their pants
the menace
of our education. It is not Dante,
nor Yeats. But the loud and drunken
pilgrim, I knew so well

in my youth. And grew to stone
waiting for the change.

2

The calendar is memory. The dead roots
of the poet's brain. Yellow skin, black
skin, or the formless calm of compromise. They will not come
to see, or understand you. They will call you "murderer,"
as new songs for their young. The mountains
in your country, the flat skies of mine. (Except
by the oceans, the poor hate their shadows,
and force their agony to dance.

All night blue leaves ring
in Kyoto. And the windows of 5th street
scream.

An Agony. As Now

I am inside someone
who hates me. I look
out from his eyes. Smell
what fouled tunes come in
to his breath. Love his
wretched women.

Slits in the metal, for sun. Where
my eyes sit turning, at the cool air
the glance of light, or hard flesh
rubbed against me, a woman, a man,
without shadow, or voice, or meaning.

This is the enclosure (flesh,
where innocence is a weapon. An
abstraction. Touch. (Not mine.
Or yours, if you are the soul I had
and abandoned when I was blind and had
my enemies carry me as a dead man
(if he is beautiful, or pitied.

It can be pain. (As now, as all his
flesh hurts me.) It can be that. Or
pain. As when she ran from me into
that forest.

                 Or pain, the mind
silver spiraled whirled against the
sun, higher than even old men thought
God would be. Or pain. And the other. The
yes. (Inside his books, his fingers. They
are withered yellow flowers and were never
beautiful.) The yes. You will, lost soul, say
'beauty.' Beauty, practiced, as the tree. The
slow river. A white sun in its wet sentences.
Or, the cold men in their gale. Ecstasy. Flesh
or soul. The yes. (Their robes blown. Their bowls
empty. They chant at my heels, not at yours.) Flesh
or soul, as corrupt. Where the answer moves too quickly.
Where the God is a self, after all.)

Cold air blown through narrow blind eyes. Flesh,
white hot metal. Glows as the day with its sun.
It is a human love, I live inside. A bony skeleton
you recognize as words or simple feeling.

But it has no feeling. As the metal, is hot, it is not,
given to love.

It burns the thing
inside it. And that thing
screams.

A POEM FOR WILLIE BEST*

I

The face sings, alone
at the top
      of the body. All
flesh, all song, aligned. For hell
is silent, at those cracked lips
flakes of skin and mind
twist and whistle softly
as they fall.
      It was your own death
you saw. Your own face, stiff
and raw. This
without sound, or
movement. Sweet afton, the
dead beggar bleeds
yet. His blood, for a time
alive, and huddled in a door
way, struggling to sing. Rain
washes it into cracks. Pits
whose bottoms are famous. Whose sides
are innocent broadcasts
of another life.

*Willie Best was a Negro character actor whose Hollywood name was Sleep'n'eat.

II

At this point, neither
front nor back. A point, the
dimensionless line. The top
of a head, seen from Christ's
heaven, stripped of history
or desire.

    Fixed, perpendicular
to shadow. (even speech, vertical,
leaves no trace. Born in to death
held fast to it, where
the lover spreads his arms, the line
he makes to threaten Gods with history.
The fingers stretch to emptiness. At
each point, after flesh, even light
is speculation. But an end, his end,
failing a beginning.

2

A cross. The gesture, symbol, line
arms held stiff, nailed stiff, with
no sign, of what gave them strength.
The point, become a line, a cross, or
the man, and his material, driven in
the ground. If the head rolls back
and the mouth opens, screamed into
existence, there will be perhaps
only the slightest hint of movement—
a smear; no help will come. No one
will turn to that station again.

III

At a cross roads, sits the
player. No drum, no umbrella, even
though it's raining. Again, and we
are somehow less miserable because
here is a hero, used to being wet.
One road is where you are standing now
(reading this, the other, crosses then
rushes into a wood.

       5 lbs neckbones.
       5 lbs hog innards.
       10 bottles cheap wine.
                      (The contents
of a paper bag, also shoes, with holes
for the big toe, and several rusted
knives. This is a literature, of
symbols. And it is his gift, as the
bag is.
      (The contents
again, holy saviours,

       300 men on horseback
       75 bibles
       the quietness
of a field. A rich
man, though wet through
by the rain.
      I said,

       47 howitzers
       7 polished horses jaws
       a few trees being waved
softly back under
the black night

All This should be
invested.

IV

Where
ever,
       he has gone. who ever
mourns
or sits silent
to remember

There is nothing of pity
here. Nothing
of sympathy.

V

This is the dance of the raised
leg. Of the hand on the knee
quickly.
            As a dance it punishes
speech. 'The house burned. The
old man killed.'
                  As a dance it
is obscure.

VI

This is the song
of the highest C.
                  The falsetto. An elegance
that punishes silence. This is the song

of the toes pointed inward, the arms swung, the
hips, moved, for fucking, slow, from side
to side. He is quoted
saying, "My father was
never a jockey,

        but

            he did teach me
            how to ride."

VII

The balance.
           (Rushed in, swarmed of dark, cloaks,
and only red lights pushed a message
to the street. Rub.
           This is the lady,
I saw you with.
This is your mother.
This is the lady I wanted
some how to sleep with.
           As a dance, or
our elegant song. Sun red and grown
from trees, fences, mud roads in dried out
river beds. This is for me, with no God
but what is given. Give me.
              Something more
than what is here. I must tell you
my body hurts.
The balance.
           Can you hear? Here
I am again. Your boy, dynamite. Can
you hear? My soul is moved. The soul
you gave me. I say, my soul, and it

is moved. That soul
you gave me.

                Yes, I'm sure
this is the lady. You
slept with her. Witness, your boy,
here, dynamite. Hear?

                    I mean
can you?

The balance.
              He was tired of losing. (And
his walking buddies tired
of walking.
          Bent slightly,
at the waist. Left hand low, to flick
quick showy jabs ala Sugar. The right
cocked, to complete,
                  any combination.
                        He was
tired of losing, but he was fighting
a big dumb "farmer."
              Such a blue bright
afternoon, and only a few hundred yards
from the beach. He said, I'm tired
of losing.
          "I *got* ta cut 'cha."

VIII

A renegade
behind the mask. And even
the mask, a renegade
disguise. Black skin
and hanging lip.

Lazy
Frightened
Thieving
Very potent sexually
Scars
Generally inferior
                              (but natural

rhythms.

His head is
at the window. The only
part
        that sings.

(The word he used
                (we are passing St. Mark's place
                and those crazy jews who fuck)
                                        to provoke

in neon, still useful
in the rain,
            to provoke
some meaning, where before
there was only hell. I said
silence, at his huddled blood.
                            It is an obscene invention.
                            A white sticky discharge.
                            "Jism," in white chalk
                            on the back of Angel's garage.
                            Red jackets with the head of
                            Hobbes staring into space. "Jasm"
                            the name the leader took, had it
                            stenciled on his chest.

                                        And he sits
wet at the crossroads, remembering distinctly
each weightless face that eases by. (Sun at
the back door, and that hideous mindless grin.

                              (Hear?

Joseph to His Brothers

They characterize
their lives, and I
fill up
with mine. Fill up
with what I have, with what
I see (or
need. I make
no distinction. As blind men
cannot love too quiet beauty.

These philosophers
rein up
their boats. Bring
their gifts, weapons
to my door. As if
that, in itself,
was courage, or counting
science.

The story is a long one. Why
I am here like this. Why you
should listen, now, so late, and
weary at the night. Its
heavy rain

pushing
the grass flat.
                    It is here
somewhere. It grows
here. Answers. Questions. Noise
as stiff as silence. Silver quiet
beaten heavy under rains. So little
of this we remember. So few portions
of our lives, go on.

SHORT SPEECH TO MY FRIENDS

A political art, let it be
tenderness, low strings the fingers
touch, or the width of autumn
climbing wider avenues, among the virtue
and dignity of knowing what city
you're in, who to talk to, what clothes
—even what buttons—to wear. I address

                              / the society
                         the image, of
                         common utopia.

                         / The perversity
                         of separation, isolation,
after so many years of trying to enter their kingdoms,
now they suffer in tears, these others, saxophones whining
through the wooden doors of their less than gracious homes.
The poor have become our creators. The black. The thoroughly
ignorant.
            Let the combination of morality
and inhumanity
begin.

2.

Is power, the enemy? (Destroyer
of dawns, cool flesh of valentines, among
the radios, pauses, drunks
of the 19th century. I see it,
as any man's single history. All the possible heroes
dead from heat exhaustion

       at the beach

       or hiding for years from cameras
only to die cheaply in the pages
of our daily lie.

     One hero
has pretensions toward literature
one toward the cultivation of errors, arrogance,
and constantly changing disguises, as trucker, boxer,
valet, barkeep, in the aging taverns of memory. Making love
to those speedy heroines of masturbation or kicking literal evil
continually down filmy public stairs.

A compromise
would be silence. To shut up, even such risk
as the proper placement
of verbs and nouns. To freeze the spit
in mid-air, as it aims itself
at some valiant intellectual's face.

There would be someone
who would understand, for whatever
fancy reason. Dead, lying, Roi, as your children
came up, would also rise. As George Armstrong Custer
these 100 years, has never made
a mistake.

THE POLITICS OF RICH PAINTERS

is something like the rest
of our doubt, whatever slow thought
comes to rest, beneath the silence
of starving talk.

                    Just their fingers' prints
staining the cold glass, is sufficient
for commerce, and a proper ruling on
humanity. You know the pity
of democracy, that we must sit here
and listen to how he made his money.
Tho the catalogue of his possible ignorance
roars and extends through the room
like fire. "Love," becomes the pass,
the word taken intimately to combat
all the uses of language. So that learning
itself falls into disrepute.

2

What they have gathered into themselves
in that short mean trip from mother's iron tit
to those faggot handmaidens of the french whore
who wades slowly in the narrows, waving her burnt out
torch. There are movies, and we have opinions. There are

regions of compromise so attractive, we daily long
to filthy our minds with their fame. And all the songs
of our handsome generation fall clanging like stones
in the empty darkness of their heads.

                              Couples, so beautiful
in the newspapers, marauders of cheap sentiment. So much taste
so little understanding, except some up and coming queer explain
cinema and politics while drowning a cigarette.

   3

They are more ignorant than the poor
tho they pride themselves with that accent. And
move easily in fake robes of egalitarianism. Meaning,
I will fuck you even if you don't like art. And are wounded
that you call their italian memories petit bourgeois.

                                       Whose death
will be Malraux's? Or the names Senghor, Price, Baldwin
whispered across the same dramatic pancakes, to let each
     eyelash flutter
at the news of their horrible deaths. It is a cheap game
to patronize the dead, unless their deaths be accountable
to your own understanding. Which be nothing nothing
if not bank statements and serene trips to our ominous
     countryside.
Nothing, if not whining talk about handsome white men. Nothing
if not false glamourous and static. Except, I admit, your lives
are hideously real.

   4

The source of their art crumbles into legitimate history.
The whimpering pigment of a decadent economy, slashed
     into life

as Yeats' mad girl plummeting over the nut house wall, her broken
knee caps rattling in the weather, reminding us of lands
our antennae do not reach.
And there are people in these savage geographies
use your name in other contexts
think, perhaps, the title of your latest painting
another name for liar.

A POEM FOR DEMOCRATS

the city rises

        in color, our sad
ness, blanket this wood place, single drop
of rain, blue image of
someone's love.
        Net of rain. Crystal ice
glass strings, smash
(on such repertoire of memory
as:
   baskets
   the long walk up harbor
   & the insistence, rain, as they build

City, is wicked. Not
this one, where I am, where they
still move, go to, out of
(transporting your loved one
across the line is death
by drowning.

       Drowned love
hanged man, swung, cement on his feet.)
                 But

the small filth of the small mind
short structures of
newark, baltimore, cincinnati, omaha. Distress,
europe has passed we are alone. Europe
frail woman dead, we are alone

THE MEASURE OF MEMORY
(THE NAVIGATOR

The presence of good
is its answer (at the curb
the dead white verb, horse
breathing white steam
in the air)
        Leaving, into the clocks
sad lovely lady fixed by words
her man
her rest
her fingers
her wooden house
set against the rocks
of our nation's
enterprise.

That we disappear
to dance, and dance
when we do,
badly.

And wield sentiment
like flesh
like the dumb man's voice

like the cold environment
of need. Or despair, a trumpet
with poison mouthpiece, blind player,
at the garden of least discernment; I
stagger, and remember / my own terrible
blankness and lies.

———————————

The boat's prow angled at the sun
Stiff foam and an invisible cargo
of captains. I buy injury, and decide
the nature of silence. Lines of speed
decay in my voice.

FOOTNOTE TO A PRETENTIOUS BOOK

Who am I to love
so deeply? As against
a heavy darkness, pressed
against my eyes. Wetting
my face, a constant trembling
rain.

     A long life, to you. My friend. I
tell that to myself, slowly, sucking
my lip. A silence of motives / empties
the day of meaning.
                        What is intimate
enough? What is
beautiful?

          It is slow unto meaning for
any life. If I am an animal, there
is proof of my living. The fawns
and calves
of my age. But it is steel that falls
as a thin mist into my consciousness. As a fine
ugly spray, I have made
some futile ethic
with.

"Changed my life?" As the dead man
pacing at the edge of the sea. As
the lips, closed
for so long, at the sight
of motionless
birds.

There is no one to entrust with
meaning. (These sails go by, these small
deadly animals.)

And meaning? These words?
Were there some blue expanse
of world. Some other
flesh, resting
at the roof
of the world . . .

you could say of me,
that I was truly
simpleminded.

Rhythm & Blues (1

for Robert Williams, in exile

The symbols hang limply
in the street. A forest of objects,
motives,
>black steaming christ
>meat wood and cars
>flesh light and stars
>scream each new dawn for

whatever leaves pushed from gentle lips
fire shouted from the loins of history
immense dream of each silence grown to punctuation
against the grey flowers of the world.

    I live against them, and hear them, and move
the way they move. Hanged against the night, so many
leaves, not even moving. The women scream tombs
and give the nights a dignity. For his heels
dragged in the brush. For his lips dry as brown wood. As
the simple motion of flesh whipping the air.

An incorrigible motive.
An action so secret it creates.
Men dancing on a beach.

Disappeared laughter erupting as the sea
erupts.
Controlled eyes seeing now all
there is
Ears that have grown
to hold their new maps
Enemies that grow
in silence
Empty white fingers
against the keys (a drunken foolish stupor
to kill these men
and scream "Economics," my God, "Economics"
for all the screaming women drunker still, laid out to rest
under the tables of nightclubs
under the thin trees of expensive forests
informed of nothing save the stink of their failure
the peacock insolence of zombie regimes
the diaphanous silence of empty churches
the mock solitude of a spastic's art.
                                    "Love." My God, (after they
scream "Economics," these shabby personalities
the pederast anarchist chants against millions of
Elk-sundays in towns quieter than his. Lunches. Smells
the sidewalk invents, and the crystal music even dumb niggers
hate. They scream it down. They will not hear your jazz. Or
let me tell of the delicate colors of the flag, the graphic blouse
of the beautiful italian maiden. Afternoon spas
with telephone booths, Butterfingers, grayhaired anonymous
    trustees.
dying with the afternoon. The people of my life
caressed with a silence that only they understand. Let their sons
make wild sounds of their mothers for your pleasure. Or

drive deep wedges in flesh / screaming birds of mourning, at
their own. The invisible mountains of New Jersey, linger
where I was born And the wind on that stone

2

Street of tinsel, and the jeweled dancers
of Belmont. Stone royalty they tear down
for new buildings where fags invent jellies.

A tub, a slick head, and the pink houses waving
at the night as it approaches. A dead fish truck
full of porters I ran track with, effeminate blues singers, the wealth
of the nation transposed into the ring of my flesh's image.
    Grand dancers
spray noise and disorder in these old tombs. Liverwurst
    sandwiches dry
on brown fenced-in lawns, unfinished cathedrals tremble with
    our screams.
Of the dozens, the razor, the cloth, the sheen, all speed adventure
    locked
in my eyes. I give you now, to love me, if I spare what flesh of yours
is left. If I see past what I feel, and call music simply "Art" and will
not take it to its logical end. For the death by hanging, for
the death by the hooded political murderer, for the old man
    dead in his
tired factory; election machines chime quietly his fraudulent faith.

For the well that marks the burned stores. For the deadly idiot
    of compromise
who shrieks compassion, and bids me love my neighbor. Even
    beyond the meaning

of such act as would give all my father's dead ash to fertilize
    their bilious
land. Such act as would give me legend, "This is the man who
    saved us
Spared us from the disappearance of the sixteenth note, the
    destruction
of the scale. This is the man who against the black pits of
    despairing genius
cried, "Save the Popular Song." For them who pat me in the
    huddle and do not
argue at the plays. For them who finish second and are happy
    they are Chinese,
and need not run those 13 blocks.
I am not moved. I will not move to save them. There is no
"melody." Only the foot stomped, the roaring harmonies of
    need. The
hand banged on the table, waved in the air. The teeth pushed
    against
the lip. The face and fingers sweating. "Let me alone," is
    praise enough
for these musicians.

3

My own mode of conscience. And guilt, always the obvious
    connection.
They spread you in the sun, and leave you there, one of a
    kind, who
has no sons to tell this to. The mind so bloated at its own
    judgment. The
railing consequence of energy given in silence. Ideas whose
    sole place

is where they form. The language less than the act. The act so
   far beyond
itself, meaning all forms, all modes, all voices, chanting for safety.

I am deaf and blind and lost and still not again sing your
   quiet verse. I have lost
even the act of poetry, and writhe now for cool horizonless
   dawn. The
shake and chant, bulled electric motion, figure of what there
   will be
as it sits beside me waiting to live past my own meekness. My own
light skin. Bull of yellow perfection, imperfectly made,
   imperfectly
understood, except as it rises against the mountains, like sun
but brighter, like flame but hotter. There will be those
who will tell you it will be beautiful.

CROW JANE

"Crow Jane, Crow Jane, don't hold your head so high,
You realize, baby, you got to lay down and die."
—Mississippi Joe Williams

FOR CROW JANE
(MAMA DEATH.

For dawn, wind
off the river. Wind
and light, from
the lady's hand. Cold
stuff, placed against
strong man's lips. Young gigolo's
of the 3rd estate. Young ruffians
without no homes. The wealth
is translated, corrected, a
dark process, like thought, tho
it provide a landscape
with golden domes.
                    "Your people
without love." And life
rots them. Makes a silence
blankness in every space
flesh thought to be. (First light,
is dawn. Cold stuff
to tempt a lover. Old lady
of flaking eyes. Moon lady
of useless thighs.

CROW JANE'S MANNER.

                Is some pilgrimage
to thought. Where she goes, in fairness,
"nobody knows." And then, without love,
returns to those wrinkled stomachs
ragged bellies / of young ladies
gone with seed. Crow
will not have. Dead virgin
of the mind's echo. Dead lady
of thinking, back now, without
the creak of memory.
                    Field is yellow. Fils dead
(Me, the last . . . black lip hung
in dawn's gray wind. The last,
for love, a taker, took my kin.

Crow. Crow. Where
you leave my
other boys?

CROW JANE IN HIGH SOCIETY.

                                    (Wipes
her nose
on the draperies. Spills drinks
fondles another man's
life. She is looking
for alternatives. Openings
where she can lay all
this greasy talk
on somebody. Me, once. Now
I am her teller.
                        (And I tell
her symbols, as the grey movement
of clouds. Leave
grey movements
of clouds. Leave, always,
more.

Where is she? That she
moves without light. Even
in our halls. Even with
our laughter, lies, dead drunk
in a slouch hat famous king.
                                    Where?

To come on so.

CROW JANE THE CROOK.

Of the night
of the rain, she
reigned, reined, her
fat whores and horse.

(A cloud burst,
and wet us. The mountain
split, and burned us. We thought
we were done.

        Jane.
Wet lady of no image. We
thought, you had left us. Dark
lady, of constant promise. We thought
you had gone.

  2.

My heart is cast in bitter
metal. Condiments, spices
all the frustration of earth,
that has so much more desire

than resolution. Want than pleasure.
Oh, Jane. (Her boat bumps at the ragged
shore. Soul of the ocean, go out, return.
Oh, Jane, we thought you had gone.

THE DEAD LADY CANONIZED.

 (A thread
of meaning. Meaning light. The quick
response. To breath, or the virgins
sick odor against the night.

 (A trail
of objects. Dead nouns, rotted faces
propose the nights image. Erect
for that lady, a grave of her own.

 (The stem
of the morning, sets itself, on
each window (of thought, where it
goes. The lady is dead, may the Gods,

 (those others
beg our forgiveness. And Damballah, kind father,
sew up
her bleeding hole.

Duncan Spoke of a Process

And what I have learned
of it, to repeat, repeated
as a day will repeat
its color, the tired sounds
run off its bones. In me, a balance.

Before that, what came easiest. From
wide poles, across the greenest earth,
eyes locked on, where they could live, and
whatever came from there, where the hand
could be offered, like Gideon's young troops
on their knees at the water.

                      I test myself,
with memory. A live bloody skeleton. Hung as softly
as summer. Sways like words' melody, as ugly as any
lips, or fingers stroking lakes, or flesh like a
white frightened scream.

What comes, closest, is
closest. Moving, there
is a wreck of spirit,
                  a heap of broken feeling. What

was only love
or in those cold rooms,
opinion. Still, it made
color. And filled me
as no one will. As, even
I cannot fill
myself.

        I see what I love most and will not
leave what futile lies
I have. I am where there
is nothing, save myself. And go out to
what is most beautiful. What some noncombatant Greek
or soft Italian prince
would sing, "Noble Friends."
                        Noble Selves. And which one

is truly
to rule here? And
what country is this?

Audubon, Drafted

for Linda

It does not happen. That love, removes
itself. (I am leaving, Goodbye!
                         Removes
itself, as rain, hard iron rain
comes down, then stops. All those
eyes opened for morning, close with
what few hours given them. With tears,
or at a stone wall, shadows drag down.

I am what I think I am. You are what
I think you are. The world is the
one thing, that will not move. It is
made of stone, round, and very ugly.

IF INTO LOVE THE IMAGE BURDENS

The front of the head
is the scarred cranium. The daisy
night, alone with its mills. Grumbling
through history, with its nest
of sorrow. I felt lost
and alone. The windows
sat on the street and smoked
in dangling winter. To autumn
from spring, summer's questions
paths, present to the head
and fingers. The shelf. The
rainbow. Cold knuckles rub against
a window. The rug. The flame. A woman
kneels against the sill. Each figure
halves silence. Each equation
sprinkles light.

Grey hats and eyes
for the photographed
trees. Grey stones and limbs
and a herd of me's.

Past, perfect.

Each correct color
not in nature, makes
us weep. Each inexpressible
idea. The fog lifts. The fog
lifts. Now falls. The fog
falls.

And nothing is done, or complete. No person
loved, or made better or beautiful. Came here
lied to, leave
the same. Dead boned talk
of history. Grandfathers skid
down a ramp of the night. Flame
for his talk, if it twists
like light on leaves.

Out past the fingers.
Out past the eyes.

BLACK DADA NIHILISMUS

.   . Against what light

is false what breath
sucked, for deadness.
                    Murder, the cleansed

purpose, frail, against
God, if they bring him
                    bleeding, I would not

forgive, or even call him
black dada nihilismus.

The protestant love, wide windows,
color blocked to Mondrian, and the
ugly silent deaths of jews under

the surgeon's knife. (To awake on
69th street with money and a hip
nose. Black dada nihilismus, for

the umbrella'd jesus. Trilby intrigue
movie house presidents sticky the floor.
B.D.N., for the secret men, Hermes, the

blacker art. Thievery (ahh, they return
those secret gold killers. Inquisitors
of the cocktail hour. Trismegistus, have

them, in their transmutation, from stone
to bleeding pearl, from lead to burning
looting, dead Moctezuma, find the West

a grey hideous space.

2

From Sartre, a white man, it gave
the last breath. And we beg him die,
before he is killed. Plastique, we

do not have, only thin heroic blades.
The razor. Our flail against them, why
you carry knives? Or brutaled lumps of

heart? Why you stay, where they can
reach? Why you sit, or stand, or walk
in this place, a window on a dark

warehouse. Where the minds packed in
straw. New homes, these towers, for those
lacking money or art. A cult of death,

need of the simple striking arm under
the streetlamp. The cutters, from under
their rented earth. Come up, black dada

nihilismus. Rape the white girls. Rape
their fathers. Cut the mothers' throats.
Black dada nihilismus, choke my friends

in their bedrooms with their drinks spilling
and restless for tilting hips or dark liver
lips sucking splinters from the master's thigh.

Black scream
and chant, scream,
and dull, un
earthly
hollering. Dada, bilious
what ugliness, learned
in the dome, colored holy
shit (i call them sinned

or lost
      burned masters
                of the lost
                        nihil German killers
                                all our learned

art, 'member
what you said
money, God, power,
a moral code, so cruel
it destroyed Byzantium, Tenochtitlan, Commanch
                            (got it, *Baby!*

For tambo, willie best, dubois, patrice, mantan, the
bronze buckaroos.

For Jack Johnson, asbestos, tonto, buckwheat,
billie holiday.
For tom russ, l'overture, vesey, beau jack,

(may a lost god damballah, rest or save us
against the murders we intend
against his lost white children
black dada nihilismus

A GUERRILLA HANDBOOK

In the palm
the seed
is burned up
in the wind.
                    In their rightness
the tree trunks are socialists
leaves murder the silence and are brown
and old when they blow to the sea.
                                        Convinced
of the lyric. Convinced
of the man's image (since
he will not look at substance
other than his ego. Flowers, grapes
the shadows of weeds, as the weather
is colder, and women walk
with their heads down.
                        Silent political rain
against the speech
of friends. (We love them
trapped in life, knowing no way out
except description. Or black soil
floating in the arm.
                        We must convince the living
                        that the dead
                        cannot sing.

GREEN LANTERN'S SOLO

A deep echo, of open fear: the field drawn in
as if to close, and die, in the old man's eyes
as if to shut itself, as the withered mouth of
righteousness beats its gums on the cooling day.
                                As if to die
                                without knowing life.
                                Having lived, when
                                he did (an old stout God
                                in the spent bones
                                of his dignity. No screams
                                break his wooden lips
                                His urine scatters
                                as steel, which will fall
                                on any soft thing
                                you have. (Murder

                                is speaking of us.

I break and run, or hang back and hide
having been killed by wild beasts in my young wife's
sleep. Having been torn into small echoes of lie, or surrounded
in dim rooms by the smelly ghosts of wounded intellectuals. Old
   science majors
                     whose mothers were brilliant understudys
               or the famous mistress of a benevolent gangster.

Some mysterious comment on the world at the birth
of the word. Some mysterious jangle of intellects bent on the
    crudeness
of any death so perfectly ignorant as ours.
                                My friend, the lyric poet,
                        who has never had an orgasm. My friend,
                    the social critic, who has never known society,
                or read the great Italian liars, except his father
who calls the whitehouse nightly, asking for hideous assignments.
My friend who has thrown himself against the dignity of all
    human flesh
yet beats at its image, as if he was the slow intellect who thought up
God.
        No, Nigger, no, blind drunk in SantaSurreal's beard.
        Dead hero
for our time who would advance the nation's economy by
    poking holes
in his arms. As golden arms build a forest of loves, and find only
the heavy belly breath of ladies whispering their false
    pregnancies through the
phone. The stagnant image of bats sailing out of their mouths
    as they
shape the syllable of revenge. Let me say it is Love, but never
    feeling.
It is knowledge, but never perfection, or something as stupidly
    callous as beauty.

2

So important a silence as their lives, dwindled, rusted,
    corrupted
away. As the port, where smoke rises for the poor french sailor
and his indian whore. There are bones, which still clog those blue

soft seas, and give a human history to nature. Can you understand
that nothing is free! Even the floating strangeness of the
    poet's head
the crafted visions of the intellect, *named, controlled,* beat and
    erected
to work, and struggle under the heavy fingers of art. What
    valley, what
mountain, what eagle or afternoon, is not fixed or changed
    under our feet
or eyes? What man unremoved from his meat's source, can
    continue
to believe totally in himself? Or on the littered sidewalks of
    his personal
history, can continue to believe in his own dignity or
    intelligence.
Except the totally ignorant
who are our leaders.

                      Except the completely devious
                      who are our lovers.

                              No man except a charlatan
                              could be called "Teacher," as

big birds will run off from their young
if they follow too closely, or the drowned youths at puberty
who did not allow that ritual was stronger than
their mother's breasts.

The completely free are the completely innocent, of which
no thing I know can claim: despite the dirty feet
of our wise men, their calm words hung in a line, from city
to city: despite the sickening courage or useless honesty
of men who claim to love each other and resolve their lives
as four letter words: despite the rightness, the strength

104

the brilliance and character, the undeniable idiocy of poets
like Marx and Rousseau.

> What we have created, is ourselves
> as heroes, as lovers, as disgustingly
> evil. As Dialogues with the soul, with
> the self, Selves, screaming furiously
> to each other. As the same fingers
> touch the same faces, as the same
> mouths close on each other. The killed
> is the killer, the loved the lover

and the islands of mankind have grown huge to include all life,
all lust, all commerce and beauty. Each idea a reflection of itself
and all the ideas men have ever had. Truth, Lie, so close they defy
inspection, and are built into autonomy by naive fools,
who have no wish for wholeness or strength. Who can not but
    yearn
for the One Mind, or Right, or call it some God, a thing beyond
themselves, some thing toward which all life is fixed, some static,
irreducible, constantly correcting, dogmatic economy

> of the soul.

WAR POEM

The battle waxed (battle wax, good night!
       Steep tumors of the sea's energy
       shells, shells, gold lights under the tree's
       cover.)

              In spring the days explode
              In spain old cuckolds watch their wives
              and send their money to America.

              Straw roofs, birds, any thing we have not
              got. Destroyed before it got here. *Battle,*
              an old dead flower she put on her breast.

              Shells crush the beach. Are crushed
              beneath her feet. Wait for night,
              and the one soldier will not mind us
              sitting here, listening to the familiar
              water, scatter in the shadows.

POLITICAL POEM

for Basil

Luxury, then, is a way of
being ignorant, comfortably
An approach to the open market
of least information. Where theories
can thrive, under heavy tarpaulins
without being cracked by ideas.

(I have not seen the earth for years
and think now possibly "dirt" is
negative, positive, but clearly
social. I cannot plant a seed, cannot
recognize the root with clearer dent
than indifference. Though I eat
and shit as a natural man (Getting up
from the desk to secure a turkey sandwich
and answer the phone: the poem undone
undone by my station, by my station,
and the bad words of Newark.) Raised up
to the breech, we seek to fill for this
crumbling century. The darkness of love,
in whose sweating memory all error is forced.

Undone by the logic of any specific death. (Old gentlemen
who still follow fires, tho are quieter

and less punctual. It is a polite truth
we are left with. Who are you? What are you
saying? Something to be dealt with, as easily.
The noxious game of reason, saying, "No, No,
you cannot feel," like my dead lecturer
lamenting thru gipsies his fast suicide.

SNAKE EYES

That force is lost
which shaped me, spent
in its image, battered, an old brown thing
swept off the streets
where it sucked its
gentle living.
              And what is meat
to do, that is driven to its end
by words? The frailest gestures
grown like skirts around breathing.
                          We take
unholy risks to prove
we are what we cannot be. For instance,

I am not even crazy.

A Poem for Speculative Hipsters

He had got, finally,
to the forest
of motives. There were no
owls, or hunters. No Connie Chatterleys
resting beautifully
on their backs, having casually
brought socialism
to England.
                    Only ideas,
and their opposites.
                              Like,
                    he was *really*
                    nowhere.

DICHTUNG

A torn body, correspondent

of extreme cold. Altitude
or thought. colliding as an image
of
moving water, time, the slip

of simple life. It is matter, after all,
that is corrupted, not
spirit. After all, it is spirit
that is corrupted
not matter.
     The role given,
mashed into protein
grace. *A* lifted arm
in shadow. A lifted thinking
banging silently
in the darkness.
       I fondle what
I find
of myself. Of you
what I understand.
       Trumpets of slow weather.
       Love blends
       in season.

Valéry as Dictator

Sad. And it comes
tomorrow. Again, gray, the streaks
of work
shedding the stone
of the pavement, dissolving
with the idea
of singular endeavor. Herds, the
herds
of suffering intelligences
bunched,
and out of
hearing. Though the day
come to us
      in waves,
             sun, air, the beat
of the clock.
        Though I stare at the radical
world,
    wishing it would stand still.
                Tell me,
and I gain at the telling.
Of the lie, and the waking
against the heavy breathing
of new light, dawn, shattering

the naive cluck
of feeling
             What is tomorrow
that it cannot come
                   today?

THE LIAR

What I thought was love
in me, I find a thousand instances
as fear. (Of the tree's shadow
winding around the chair, a distant music
of frozen birds rattling
in the cold.
                         Where ever I go to claim
my flesh, there are entrances
of spirit. And even its comforts
are hideous uses I strain
to understand.
                         Though I am a man
who is loud
on the birth
of his ways. Publicly redefining
each change in my soul, as if I had predicted
them,
          and profited, biblically, even tho
          their chanting weight,
                                             erased familiarity
                                             from my face.
                                                       A question I think,
an answer, whatever sits
counting the minutes
till you die.

When they say, "It is Roi
who is dead?" I wonder
who will they mean?

BLACK MAGIC
1969

THREE MODES OF HISTORY AND CULTURE

Chalk mark sex of the nation, on walls we drummers
know
as cathedrals. Cathedra, in a churning meat milk.

Women glide through looking for telephones. Maps
weep
and are mothers and their daughters listening to

music teachers. From heavy beginnings. Plantations,
learning
America, as speech, and a common emptiness. Songs knocking

inside old women's faces. Knocking through cardboard trunks.
Trains
leaning north, catching hellfire in windows, passing through

the first ignoble cities of missouri, to illinois, and the panting
Chicago.
And then all ways, we go where flesh is cheap. Where factories

sit open, burning the chiefs. Make your way! Up through fog and
history
Make your way, and swing the general, that it come flash open

and spill the innards of that sweet thing we heard, and gave theory
to.
Breech, bridge, and reach, to where all talk is energy. And there's

enough, for anything singular. All our lean prophets and rhythms.
Entire
we arrive and set up shacks, hole cards, Western hearts at the edge

of saying. Thriving to balance the meanness of particular skies.
Race
of madmen and giants.

Brick songs. Shoe songs. Chants of open weariness.
Knife wiggle early evenings of the wet mouth. Tongue
dance midnight, any season shakes our house. Don't
tear my clothes! To doubt the balance of misery
ripping meat hug shuffle fuck. The Party of Insane
Hope. I've come from there too. Where the dead told lies
about clever social justice. Burning coffins voted
and staggered through cold white streets listening
to Willkie or Wallace or Dewey through the dead face
of Lincoln. Come from there, and belched it out.

I think about a time when I will be relaxed.
When flames and non-specific passion wear themselves
away. And my eyes and hands and mind can turn
and soften, and my songs will be softer
and lightly weight the air.

A Poem Welcoming Jonas Mekas
to America

This night's first star, hung
high up over a factory. From my window,
a smile held my poetry in. A tower, where I work
and drink, vomit, and spoil myself for casual life.

Looking past things, to their meanings. All the pretensions
of consciousness. Looking out, or in, the precise stare
of painful reference. (Saying to the pretty girl, "Pain
has to be educational.") Or so I thought, riding down

in the capsule, call it elevator lady, speedless forceless
profile thrust toward the modern lamp, in lieu of a natural
sun. Our beings are here. (Take this chance to lick yourself,
the salt and stain of memory history and object.) Shit! Love!

Things we must have some use for. Old niggers in time on the
dreary street. Man, 50 . . . woman, 50, drunk and falling in the
    street.
I could say, looking at their lot, a poet has just made a note of your
hurt. First star, high over the factory. I could say, if I had any
    courage

but my own. First star, high over the factory. Get up off the
    ground, or
just look at it, calmly, where you are.

A Poem Some People Will Have to Understand

Dull unwashed windows of eyes
and buildings of industry. What
industry do I practice? A slick
colored boy, 12 miles from his
home. I practice no industry.
I am no longer a credit
to my race. I read a little,
scratch against silence slow spring
afternoons.

      I had thought, before, some years ago
that I'd come to the end of my life.

      Watercolor ego. Without the preciseness
a violent man could propose.

      But the wheel, and the wheels,
wont let us alone. All the fantasy
      and justice, and dry charcoal winters
All the pitifully intelligent citizens
      I've forced myself to love.

      We have awaited the coming of a natural
phenomenon. Mystics and romantics,
   knowledgeable
workers
of the land.

But none has come.
(Repeat)
But none has come.

Will the machinegunners please step forward?

LETTER TO E. FRANKLIN FRAZIER

Those days when it was all right
to be a criminal, or die, a postman's son,
full of hallways and garbage, behind the hotdog store
or in the parking lots of the beautiful beer factory.

Those days I rose through the smoke of chilling Saturdays
hiding my eyes from the shine boys, my mouth and my flesh
from their sisters. I walked quickly and always alone
watching the cheap city like I thought it would swell
and explode, and only my crooked breath could put it
together again.

By the projects and small banks of my time. Counting my steps
on tar or new pavement, following the sun like a park. I imagined
a life, that was realer than speech, or the city's anonymous
fish markets. Shuddering at dusk, with a mile or so up the hill

to get home, who did you love
then, Mussolini? What were you thinking,
Lady Day? A literal riddle of image
was me, and my smell was a continent
of familiar poetry. Walking the long way,
always the long way, and up the steep hill.

Those days like one drawn-out song, monotonously
promising. The quick step, the watchful march march,
All were leading here, to this room, where memory
stifles the present. And the future, my man, is long
time gone.

THE PEOPLE BURNING

May-Day! May-Day!
—Pilot talk

They now gonna make us shut up. Ease
thru windows in eight dollar hats
sharpening their pencils on match books. List
our errors and lies, stumbling over our souls
in the dark, for the sake of unnatural advantage.

They now gonna line you up, ask you about God. Nail
your answers on the wall, for the bowling alley owners
to decide. They now gonna pretend they flowers. Snake stalked
large named vegetables, who have, if nothing else,
the title: World's Vilest Living Things.

The Dusty Hearts of Texas, whose most honest world
is the long look into darkness, sensing the glittering
affront of reason or faith or learning. Preferring
fake tiger smells rubbed on the balls, and clothes
the peasants of no country on earth would ever be
vulgar enough to wear. The legacy of diseased mediocrity.

Become an Italian or Jew. Forget the hatred of natural
insolence. The teetering sense of right, as balance, each
natural man must have. Become a Jew, and join the union,
forget about Russia or any radicalism past a hooked grin.
Become an Italian quietist in some thin veneer of reasonable

126

gain. Lodi, Metuchen, Valley Stream, welcomes you into its
leather ridiculousness. Forget about any anarchy except the
understandable urge to be violent, or flashy, or fast, or
heavy fisted. Sing at Radio City, but never rage at the chosen,
for they have given you the keys to their hearts. Made you
the Fridays and Saturdays of the regime, clothed you in promise
and utility, and banned your thinkers to worship the rags
of your decline.

For the Reconstruction, for the march into any anonymous
        America,
stretches beyond hills of newsprint, and dishonorable intention.
Forget any dignity, but that that is easily purchased. And
        recognized
by Episcopalians as they pay their garbage bills. The
        blueprint's sound.

And the nation is smaller and the loudest mouths are recognized
and stunned by the filth of their hopeless truths. (I've got to
figure this all out. Got to remember just where I came in.
        Freedom Suite,
some five six years ago, Rollins cradling the sun, as it rose, and we
dreamed then, of becoming, unlike our fathers, and the other
        cowboys,
strong men in our time, raging and clawing, at fools of any
        persuasion.)

Now they ask me to be a jew or italian, and turn from the moment
disappearing into the shaking clock of treasonable safety, like
        reruns
of films, with sacred coon stars. To retreat, and replay; throw
        my mind out,
sit down and brood about the anachronistic God, they will tell you

is real. Sit down and forget it. Lean on your silence, breathing
the dark. Forget your whole life, pop your fingers in a closed room,
hopped-up witch doctor for the cowards of a recent generation.
   It is
choice, now, like a philosophy problem. It is choice, now, and
the weight is specific and personal. It is not an emotional decision.
There are facts, and who was it said, that this is a scientific century.

Death Is Not as Natural
As You Fags Seem to Think

I hunt
the black puritan.

          (Half-screamer

in dull tones
of another forest.

Respecter of power. That it transform, and enlarge
Hierarchy crawls over earth (change exalting space
Dried mud to mountain, cape and whip, swirled
Walkers, and riders and flyers.
Language spread into darkness. Be Vowel
                          and value
                  Consonant
                     and direction.
Rather the lust of the thing
than across to droop at its energies. In melted snows
the leather cracks, and pure men claw at their bodies.
Women laugh delicately, delicately rubbing their thighs.

And the dead king laughs, looking out the hole
in his tomb. Seeing the poor
singing his evil songs.

THE SUCCESS

Among things with souls, find me.
                    Picking thru the alphabet
                    or leaning out the window. (Lives
                    and magic.) Old witch city, the
                    lights and roads (floating) up near the tops
                    of buildings. Electric names, which are not
                    love's. A rolling Eastern distress. Water cutting
                    the coast, lulling the mysterious classes.

Murderers humming under the window.

A strutting long headed Negro. Beneath the red silk

of unique social fantasy. Shore invisible under tenements.

The Jew who torments Hitler in Paradise, wiping thick fingers

on a hospital cloth. His fingerprints on the dough, marking it

before baking. Drifting to sleep in Pelham, fucking a female spy.

This man was used against me,
in a dream.

Broken teeth
Dirty apron
Hires a bowery desperado,

        to pull out the garbage
        and imagine the whiteness
        of his wife's withered stomach.

—

Ding

—

    The proportion of Magic
has seeped so low.

    For the 1st person plural

    America, then,
        Atlantis,
            in blind overdose.

THE NEW WORLD

The sun is folding, cars stall and rise
beyond the window. The workmen leave
the street to the bums and painters' wives
pushing their babies home. Those who realize
how fitful and indecent consciousness is
stare solemnly out on the emptying street.
The mourners and soft singers. The liars,
and seekers after ridiculous righteousness. All
my doubles, and friends, whose mistakes cannot
be duplicated by machines, and this is all of our
arrogance. Being broke or broken, dribbling
at the eyes. Wasted lyricists, and men
who have seen their dreams come true, only seconds
after they knew those dreams to be horrible conceits
and plastic fantasies of gesture and extension,
shoulders, hair and tongues distributing misinformation
about the nature of understanding. No one is that simple
or priggish, to be alone out of spite and grown strong
in its practice, mystics in two-pants suits. Our style,
and discipline, controlling the method of knowledge.
Beatniks, like Bohemians, go calmly out of style. And boys
are dying in Mexico, who did not get the word.
The lateness of their fabrication: mark their holes

with filthy needles. The lust of the world. This will not
be news. The simple damning lust,

> float flat magic in low changing
> evenings. Shiver your hands
> in dance. Empty all of me for
> knowing, and will the danger
> of identification,

Let me sit and go blind in my dreaming
and be that dream in purpose and device.

A fantasy of defeat, a strong strong man
older, but no wiser than the defect of love.

The Burning General

Smoke seeping from my veins. Loss from
the eyes. Seeing winter throw its wind
around. Hoping for more, than I'll ever
have. Forgetting my projects, and the projected
sense of order, any claim to "sense" must make.
The reason Allen and the others (even freakish
pseudo dada mama) in the money jungle of controlled
pederasty
               finally bolted. Shut and gone, at the same time.

But can we replace the common exchange of experience with
    stroking
some skinny girl's penis? Is sense to be lost, all of it, so that
we can walk up Mulberry Street without getting beat up in
    Italian.

Violence and repression. Silly Nigger hatred for the
silk band of misery. They are right, those farty doctors. Perhaps
it is best to ease into kill-heaven than have no heaven at all.
What do you think, Eddie, out there in Idaho shivering against
the silence, the emptiness of straight up America? What's it
    look like
there?

Can we ask a man to savor the food of oppression? Even
if it's rich and full of mysterious meaning. Can you establish
(and that word must give my whole game away) any kind of
    equality?
Can there be such thing forced on the world? That is, that the poor
and their owners appreciate light wherever they are, simply as
    light.
Why are you so sophisticated? You used to piss and shit in
    your pants.
Now you walk around *thinking* all the time, as if that sacred act
would rewrite the world in bop talk, giving medals to every
    limping coon
in creation.

Is there more to it than that? This is the time to ask, even
    while perfecting
your line. We realize that ends and means should be
    separated, but who
will do the separating? The evaluating. You want your
    experience
thought of as valuable. Which is, listen baby, only another kind
of journalistic enterprise. Not worthy of that bumpy madness
crawled up your thighs when the urine dried those sweet lost
    winters,
and tears were the whole fucking world.

TONE POEM

for Elvin Jones and Bob Thompson

A host of loves is the city, and its memory
dead sense traveling (from England) on the sea
for two hundred years. The travelers show up in Japan
to promote peace and prosperity, perhaps a piece
of that nation's ass. Years later, years later,
plays rework the rime of lust. As history, and a cloud
their faces bang invisible notes, wind scribbled leaves
and foam. An eagle hangs above them spinning. Years and
    travelers
linger among the dead, no reports, gunshots white puffs
deciding the season and the mode of compromise. The
    general good
has no troops or armor, subtly the books stand closed, except
sad facts circled for unknown hippies carrying the mail.
I leave it there, for them, full of hope, and hurt. All the poems
are full of it. Shit and hope, and history. Read this line
young colored or white and know I felt the twist of dividing
memory. Blood spoiled in the air, caked and anonymous.
    Arms opening,
opened last night, we sat up howling and kissing. Men who
    loved
each other. Will that be understood? That we could, and still
move under cold nights with clenched fists. Swing these losers

by the tail. Got drunk then high, then sick, then quiet. But
    thinking
(and of you lovely shorties sit in libraries seeking such ideas
    out).
I'm here now, LeRoi, who tried to say something long for you.
    Keep it.
Forget me, or what I say, but not the tone, and exit image. No
    points,
or theories, from now on, just me and mine, when they get
    me, just
think of me as typing with a drink at my right hand, some
    women who
love me . . . and the day growing old and sloppy through the
    window.

Gatsby's Theory of Aesthetics

Verse, as a form, is artificial. Poetry is not a form, but rather a result. Whatever the matter, its meaning, if precise enough in its information (and direction) of the world, is poetic. The poetic is the value of poetry, and any concatenation of elements is sufficient to induce the poetic. What you see is as valuable as what you do not. But it is not as meaningful (to you). Poetry aims at difficult meanings. Meanings not already catered to. Poetry aims at reviving, say, a sense of meaning, or meaning's possibility and ubiquitousness.

Identification can be one term of that possibility. That is, showing a thing with its meaning apparent through the act of that showing. Interpretation can be another term. That is, supporting a meaning, with one's own life. That is, under, standing. And using that position as a map, or dictionary. Depending on whether you move or sit.

I write poetry only to enlist the poetic consistently as apt description of my life. I write poetry only in order to feel, and that, finally, sensually, all the terms of my life. I write poetry to investigate my self, and my meaning and meanings.

But also to invest the world with a clearer understanding of it self, but only by virtue of my having brought some clearer understanding of my self into it. I wrote in a poem once, "Feeling predicts intelligence."

But it is possible to feel with any part of our consciousness. Whatever part of us does register: whatever. The head feels. The heart feels. The penis feels. The penis is also, because it is able to feel, conscious, and has intelligence of its own. No one can deny that intelligence, or at least no one should try. The point of life is that it is arbitrary, except in its basest forms. Arbitrariness, or self imposed meaning, is the only thing worth living for. It is the only thing that permits us to live.

The only time I am conscious of my limitations is when I am writing. The rest of the time, there is no standard, at all reasonable, for judging, in fact, what limitations are.

Year of the Buffalo
1964

ALL'S WELL

for E.R. &MB.

African in the Bush of the Hatreds. One gone.

An old time love withered, in seeing, off and on
in a thing like rain (the wetness in your head, and
all the stampeding, fear, hacked open skulls grinning
sensing your loss, the words floating just beyond your
fingers (invisible antennae

Just drew a blank, dope nod
corrupting what's left, and that nothing
confusion of blankness, the hatred when I wake
silence for motives, she, woman I am with, is
silent, as the dream of some other woman, never
existed, tho she be of flesh and red sperm spinning
through her veins. This woman came when I stuck her
iron insect screams holes. Blood flew up into the
dropper, we sent it back in her. Eyes rolled up,
lap quivered, lip shook. The next time she
got depressed going cross town. She held me so.
Not understanding the buildings stopped, and sky
hung above them just the same

THE BRONZE BUCKAROO

for Herb Jeffries

Soft night comes back
with its clangs and dreams. Back
in through the base
of the hairy skull. The heavy pictures, unavailable
solaces, emptying their churchy magic
out. Golden girls, and thin black ones
patrol the dreamer's meat. Things
shovel themselves, from where they always are. Spinning, a
moment's indecision, past the vision of stealth and silence
Byron thought the night could be. Death blow Eliot silence,
    dwindling
away, in the 20th century. Poet clocks crouched in their Americas.
Dreaming of poems, only the cold sky could bring. Not room
    poems, or
fireplace poems, or the great washed poetry of our dizzy
    middleclass.
But something creeps and grabs them, rapes them on the
    pavement. The Screams
are not essays, rich blonde poetess from the mysteries of
    Kipling's harmon
nica! Not guileful treatises of waste and desire, stuck somewhere
nursing her tilted beauty, like some old fashion whore,
    embarrassed
by God, or his diseases. The funny heart blows smoke, in the winter

and gives us all the earth we need. In summer, it sweats, and
   remembers.
Half way up the hill the mutineers stand, and seek their
   comrades out.
I am half way up, and standing.

Numbers, Letters

If you're not home, where
are you? Where'd you go? What
were you doing when gone? When
you come back, better make it good.
What was you doing down there, freakin' off
with white women, hangin' out
with Queens, say it straight to be
understood straight, put it flat and real
in the street where the sun comes and the
moon comes and the cold wind in winter
waters your eyes. Say what you mean, dig
it out put it down, and be strong
about it.

I cant say who I am
unless you agree I'm real

I cant be anything I'm not
Except these words pretend
to life not yet explained,
so here's some feeling for you
see how you like it, what it
reveals, and that's Me.

Unless you agree I'm real
that I can feel
whatever beats hardest
at our black souls
I am real, and I can't say who
I am. Ask me if I know, I'll say
yes, I might say no. Still, ask.
I'm Everett LeRoi Jones, 30 yrs old.

A black nigger in the universe. A long breath singer,
wouldbe dancer, strong from years of fantasy
and study. All this time then, for what's happening
now. All that spilling of white ether, clocks in ghostheads
lips drying and rewet, eyes opening and shut, mouths churning.

I am a meditative man, And when I say something it's all of me
saying, and all the things that make me, have formed me,
    colored me
this brilliant reddish night. I will say nothing that I feel is
lie, or unproven by the same ghostclocks, by the same riders
always move so fast with the word slung over their backs or
in saddlebags, charging down Chinese roads. I carry some
    words,
some feeling, some life in me. My heart is large as my mind
this is a messenger calling, over here, over here, open your eyes
and your ears and your souls; today is the history we must learn
to desire. There is no guilt in love.

RED EYE

for Calvin Hernton and Ishmael Reed

The corrupt madness of the individual. You cannot live
alone. You are in the world. World, fuck them. World rise
and twist like you do, night madness in rain as heavy as stones.
Alabama gypsy talk, for peeling lips. Look in your mother's head,
if you really want to know everything. Your sister's locked up
pussy. Invasion of the idea syndrome like hand clapping
    winter in.
Winter will make you move. Or you will freeze in Russia and
never live to see Napoleon as conceived by Marlon Brando.
We are at the point where death is too good for us. We are
in love with the virtue of evil. This communication. Rapping
on wet meat windows, they spin in your head, if I kill you
will not even have chance to hate me

A Western Lady

The sick tightening. Brain damage movie
of forbidden flesh, laying in the shadows
breathing without purpose, meat stacked
in terrible silence, her mother wept
to think of that meat, her father, paced
and said the star spangled banner into
his brain damage soup. These were windows
we looked through. The brother died in a
guitar school, stringing guitars and praying
for a piece. And it was his own movie star
slipping green panties over high heels. Hence
his pimples, and the bunching of his waistband.
No one is expected to be rich *and* smart. Hence
planes go down from 30,000, full of screaming
materialists, whose mothers stunted them
hanging around election machines. It was the metal clack
that did it. A flag lobotomy, which has the victims
wallowing on warehouse floors, whistling popular Bach.
I suffer with these announcers. Butter and egg men,
whose promise rolled with the big ice, them's pre-
historic times.

RETURN OF THE NATIVE

Harlem is vicious
modernism. BangClash.
Vicious the way its made.
Can you stand such beauty?
So violent and transforming.
The trees blink naked, being
so few. The women stare
and are in love with them
selves. The sky sits awake
over us. Screaming
at us. No rain.
Sun, hot cleaning sun
drives us under it.

The place, and place
meant of
black people. Their heavy Egypt.
(Weird word!) Their minds, mine,
the black hope mine. In Time.
We slide along in pain or too
happy. So much love
for us. All over, so much of
what we need. Can you sing
yourself, your life, your place

on the warm planet earth.
And look at the stones
the hearts, the gentle hum
of meaning. Each thing, life
we have, or love, is meant
for us in a world like this.
Where we may see ourselves
all the time. And suffer
in joy, that our lives
are so familiar.

BLACK ART

Poems are bullshit unless they are
teeth or trees or lemons piled
on a step. Or black ladies dying
of men leaving nickel hearts
beating them down. Fuck poems
and they are useful, wd they shoot
come at you, love what you are,
breathe like wrestlers, or shudder
strangely after pissing. We want live
words of the hip world live flesh &
coursing blood. Hearts Brains
Souls splintering fire. We want poems
like fists beating niggers out of Jocks
or dagger poems in the slimy bellies
of the owner-jews. Black poems to
smear on girdlemamma mulatto bitches
whose brains are red jelly stuck
between 'lizabeth taylor's toes. Stinking
Whores! We want "poems that kill."
Assassin poems, Poems that shoot
guns. Poems that wrestle cops into alleys
and take their weapons leaving them dead
with tongues pulled out and sent to Ireland. Knockoff
poems for dope selling wops or slick halfwhite

politicians Airplane poems, rrrrrrrrrrrrrrrr
rrrrrrrrrrrrrrr . . . tuhtuhtuhtuhtuhtuhtuhtuhtuh
. . . rrrrrrrrrrrrrrrr . . . Setting fire and death to
whities ass. Look at the Liberal
Spokesman for the jews clutch his throat
& puke himself into eternity . . . rrrrrrrr
There's a negroleader pinned to
a bar stool in Sardi's eyeballs melting
in hot flame Another negroleader
on the steps of the white house one
kneeling between the sheriff's thighs
negotiating cooly for his people.
Agggh . . . stumbles across the room . . .
Put it on him, poem. Strip him naked
to the world! Another bad poem cracking
steel knuckles in a jewlady's mouth
Poem scream poison gas on beasts in green berets
Clean out the world for virtue and love,
Let there be no love poems written
until love can exist freely and
cleanly. Let Black People understand
that they are the lovers and the sons
of lovers and warriors and sons
of warriors Are poems & poets &
all the loveliness here in the world

We want a black poem. And a
Black World.
Let the world be a Black Poem
And Let All Black People Speak This Poem
Silently
or LOUD

Poem for HalfWhite College Students

Who are you, listening to me, who are you
listening to yourself? Are you white or
black or does that have anything to do
with it? Can you pop your fingers to no
music, except those wild monkies go on
in your head, can you jerk, to no melody,
except finger poppers get it together
when you turn from starchecking to checking
yourself. How do you sound, your words, are they
yours? The ghost you see in the mirror, is it really
you, can you swear you are not an imitation greyboy,
can you look right next to you in that chair, and swear,
that the sister you have your hand on is not really
so full of Elizabeth Taylor, Richard Burton is
coming out of her ears. You may even have to be Richard
with a white shirt and face, and four million negroes
think you cute, you may have to be Elizabeth Taylor, old lady,
if you want to sit up in your crazy spot dreaming about dresses,
and the sway of certain porters' hips. Check yourself, learn
   who it is
speaking, when you make some ultrasophisticated point,
   check yourself,
when you find yourself gesturing like Steve McQueen, check
   it out, ask

in your black heart who it is you are, and is that image black
   or white,

you might be surprised right out the window, whistling dixie
   on the way in.

American Ecstasy

"Loss of Life or Both Feet or Both Hands or Both Eyes . . . . The Principal Sum

Loss of One Hand and One Foot . . . . The Principal Sum

Loss of One Hand and One Eye or One Foot and One Eye . . . . The Principal Sum

Loss of One Hand or One Foot . . . . One half The Principal Sum

Loss of One Eye . . . . One fourth The Principal Sum"

153

Are Their Blues Singers In Russia?

Spies are found wanting. They wanted
in line, on the snow, a love to get high
with, and not, the line, a lie, a circling
tone of merciless involvement, the pushing, the
stomping, an image of green space was what the spy
wanted, standing there being shoved and hurled around
by his nostrils. They cold nights, after waiting, and
worse mornings. When the girls go by, and the lights go off
and on, to forget the clocks, and the counting of cobblestones
to keep pure cellar static off his back. The li'l darling, holding
'is wee wee he gotta pee, a little run down he leg. He pants soiled,
the wind freezed that part of his leg that wanted love most

We stand for tragic emblems when we return to the pros and cons
of the world. The shielding, for nothing. God's contradictions we
speak about as if we knew something, or could feel past what we
describe, and enter the new forms of being. See the door and
        enter,
get in out of the snow, the watermoccasins, and stuff, mud he
carried around in his mouth, or on the ground up to his ankles,
it'll get stupid or boring. So much, so much, to prepare a proper
place, to not exist in.

The day was a bargain.
A jew on the corner was thinking

of bargains. A dog, out back
did not start yet, howling, puny words,
barking in sorrow, a boat, for the spy's family to ride in
while they watched a sinking image of the world, and the spy's
    death
in snow they could really dig as beautiful or cool or somewhere else,
or just grimy lace curtains would make them hang against the
    boat's window
dreaming of God. The disappointment would come
after they opened their mouths, or version last
would come, and coparmies would salute the jewish dog
barking the rhythms of embezzled deserts.

We are all spies for god.

We can get betrayed. We ask for it, we ask
so much. And expect the fire the sun set the horizon
to slide through human speech dancing our future dimensions.
We expect some real shit. We expect to love all the things
somebody runs down to us. We want things, and are locked
    here, to the earth,
by pussy chains, or money chains, or personal indulgence
    chains, lies, weak
phone calls, attempts to fly when we know good and fucking
    well we can't and even
the nerve to get mad, and walk around pretending we are
    huge magnets for the
most beautiful force in the universe. And we are, but not in
    the image of wind
spreading the grass, or brown grass dying from a sudden
    snow, near the unemploy-
ment office where the spy stands trying to remember just why
    he wanted to
be the kinda spy he was

HARD FACTS

1972

History on Wheels

Civil Rights
included Nathan
and the rest
of them, who got in america
big shotting off the agony
a class of blue Bloods, hip
to the swing and sway of
the usa. yeh all the 1st
negroes world wide, joined
knees, and shuffled heroically
into congress, city hall, the
anti-p program, and a thousand
penetrable traps of cookstove
america. a class of exploiters,
in black face, collaborators,
not puppets, pulling their own
strings, and ours too, in the
poor people's buck dance, w /o
the bux. But see, then later,
you talkin afrika, and its unity
like a giant fist of iron, smashing
"racialism," around the world. But see
that fist, any fist, reared back to
strike an enemy, shd strike the real

enemy. Not a colorless shadow for
black militants in residence, to
bloat the pockets and consolidate
the power of an international
bourgeoisie. In rag time, slanting
stick legs, with a pocket full of
toasted seaweed, and a bibliography
of bitter neocapitalists or bohemian
greys, celebrating life in a dark garage
w/ all cars banned until the voodoo car
appear. The way the rich blackies showed
after we marched and built their material
base, now niggers are left in the middle
of the panafrikan highway, babbling about
eternal racism, and divine white supremacy
a hundred thousand dollar a year oppression
and now the intellectualization, the militant
resource of the new class, its historical
valorization. Between them, john johnson
and elijah, david rockefeller rests his
smiling head.

DAS KAPITAL

Strangling women in the suburban bush
they bodies laid around rotting while martinis are drunk
the commuters looking for their new yorkers feel a draft
& can get even drunker watching the teevee later on the Ford
replay. There will be streams of them coming, getting off
near where the girls got killed. Two of them strangled by
the maniac.
There are maniacs hidden everywhere cant you see? By the dozens
and double dozens, maniacs by the carload (tho they are
a minority). But they terrorize us uniformly, all over the place
we look at the walls of our houses, the garbage cans parked full
strewn around our defaulting cities, and we cd get scared. A rat
eases past us on his way to a banquet, can you hear the cheers
    raised
through the walls, full of rat humor. Blasts of fire, some
    woman's son will stumble
and dies with a pool of blood around his head. But it wont be
    the maniac. These old houses
crumble, the unemployed stumble by us straining, ashy
    fingered, harassed. The air is cold
winter heaps above us consolidating itself in degrees. We need
    a aspirin or something, and
pull our jackets close. The baldhead man on the television set
    goes on in a wooden way

his unappetizing ignorance can not be stood, or understood.
    The people turn the channel
looking for Good Times and get a negro with a pulldown hat.
    Flashes of maniac shadows before
bed, before you pull down the shade you can see the leaves
    being blown down the street
too dark now to see the writing on them, the dates, and
    amounts we owe. The streets too
will soon be empty, after the church goers go on home having
    been saved again from the
Maniac . . . except a closeup of the chief mystic's face rolling
    down to his hands will send
shivers through you, looking for traces of the maniacs life.
    Even there among the mythophrenics.

What can you do? It's time finally to go to bed. The shadows
    close around and the room is still.
Most of us know there's a maniac loose. Our lives a jumble of
    frustrations and unfilled
capacities. The dead girls, the rats noise, the flashing somber
    lights, the dead voice on
television, was that blood and hair beneath the preacher's
    fingernails? A few other clues

we mull them over as we go to sleep, the skeletons of
    dollarbills, traces of dead used up
labor, lead away from the death scene until we remember a
    quiet fit that everywhere
is the death scene. Tomorrow you got to hit it sighs through
    us like the wind, we got to
hit it, like an old song at radio city, working for the yanqui
    dollarrrr, when we were

children, and then we used to think it was not the wind, but
the maniac scratching against
our windows. Who is the maniac, and why everywhere at the
same time . . .

REAL LIFE

Ted, Ted? In the bay at the bottom of the wat
er lies the president of the united states,
his chappaqui
dick, bent around an immigrant in an
automobile. Nixon calls from the coast, you thought
you'd get away clean, but my vengeance
comes from beyond the grave.
Nixon slobbers on the phone, wetting the cocaine on the desk
he and pat have been snorting since
early morning, herb alpert blurting low contradictions in the
    wings
Shadows gather on the windows, then blow twisted into the
    whole dark
which comes now. The lights go on
in the white house. Ford cracking his knuckles
turns off the tv and calls nixon
you alright dick, he says, white whistles jag at nixons calm, high
and wild, pat's jaws quivering, green and blues come off the
    screen
and stutter 3-D in the room, sympathetic and wanting to rub them
he cant speak
rockefeller's talking
ford says the plan, was national
unity, the new money

and the old,

he cant speak, nixon cant, high, and hot, cripple forever upstairs

pat starts to pee on the rug, and roll in it. Her giggles like a
vincent

price movie, without popcorn, nixon slobbers, trying to make
a point, ford

is saying national unity, as rockefeller grins, his finger, shoving
up into

the air, across a thousand miles, at the mad western capitalists
and their

southern friends. Yall dont know how, this shit works, he is
saying (really)

the commentator, looks over his shoulder, as if he knows that
nixon is

watching. Ford whispers numbly, dick, dick, yes,

mr. president?

Horatio Alger Uses Scag

Kissinger has made it, yall. He's the secretary
of state, U.S.A. The anglo-snakes have called him
mooing to their side, his bag-time with rocky helped
a lot. His ol lady, was once, they say, rocky's main
squeeze . . . intellectually. But Henry, the k, pushes through
his dangerous glasses. His wine smile sloshes back and forth
he's thinking, as he speaks. A fast man on his feet. The subject,
a cold threat to the a-rabs (it makes him feel vaguely nationalistic,
but not in an irresponsible way, him bein a jew and all
ya know . . . but they hired him not for his jewishness
    "grrr . . . he sd
what is that", but for his absolute mastery of the art of
bullshitting.
And so, he lays it all out
across the U.N. decks for all
to hear, and be afraid. His freckles, even,
show, so synonomous with america is this
fat priapic mackman
A-rabs, he says, you betta
be cool with that oil & shit
& beyond us all, you cdda laught
is the realization that the shadowy figure
in the arab getup, is yo man, rocky, makin
                the whole thing
                  perfect

When We'll Worship Jesus

We'll worship Jesus
When jesus do
Somethin
When jesus blow up
the white house
or blast nixon down
when jesus turn out congress
or bust general motors to
yard bird motors
jesus we'll worship jesus
when jesus get down
when jesus get out his yellow lincoln
w/the built in cross stain glass
window & box w/black peoples
enemies we'll worship jesus when
he get bad enough to at least scare
somebody—cops not afraid
of jesus
pushers not afraid
of jesus, capitalists racists
imperialists not afraid
of jesus shit they makin money
off jesus
we'll worship jesus when mao

do, when toure does
when the cross replaces Nkrumah's
star
Jesus need to hurt some a our
enemies, then we'll check him
out, all that screaming and hollering
& wallering and moaning talkin bout
jesus, jesus, in a red
check velvet vine + 8 in. heels
jesus pinky finger
got a goose egg ruby
which actual bleeds
jesus at the apollo
doin splits and helpin
nixon trick niggers
jesus w/his one eyed self
tongue kissing johnny carson
up the behind
jesus need to be busted
jesus need to be thrown down and whipped
till something better happen
jesus aint did nothin for us
but kept us turned toward the
sky (him and his boy allah
too, need to be checkd
out!)
we'll worship jesus
when he get a boat load of ak-47s
and some dynamite
and blow up abernathy robotin
for gulf
jesus need to be busted
we ain't gonna worship nobody

but niggers gettin up off
the ground
not gon worship jesus
unless he just a tricked up
nigger somebody named
outside his race
need to worship yo self fo
you worship jesus
need to bust jesus (+ check
out his spooky brother
allah while you heavy
on the case
cause we ain gon worship jesus
we aint gon worship
jesus
we aint gon worship
jesus
not till he do somethin
not till he help us
not till the world get changed
and he ain, jesus ain, he cant change the world
we can change the world
we can struggle against the forces of backwardness, we can
    change the world
we can struggle against our selves, our slowness, our
    connection with
the oppressor, the very cultural aggression which binds us to
    our enemies
as their slaves.
we can change the world
we aint gonna worship jesus cause jesus dont exist
xcept in song and story except in ritual and dance, except in
    slum stained

tears or trillion dollar opulence stretching back in history, the
    history
of the oppression of the human mind
we worship the strength in us
we worship our selves
we worship the light in us
we worship the warmth in us
we worship the world
we worship the love in us
we worship our selves
we worship nature
we worship ourselves
we worship the life in us, and science, and knowledge, and
    transformation
of the visible world
but we aint gonna worship no jesus
we aint gonna legitimize the witches and devils and spooks
    and hobgoblins
the sensuous lies of the rulers to keep us chained to fantasy
    and illusion
sing about life, not jesus
sing about revolution, not no jesus
stop singing about jesus,
sing about, creation, our creation, the life of the world and
    fantastic
nature how we struggle to transform it, but dont victimize our
    selves by
distorting the world
stop moanin about jesus, stop sweatin and crying and stompin
    and dyin for jesus
unless thats the name of the army we building to force the
    land finally to
change hands. And lets not call that jesus, get a quick
    consensus, on that,

lets damn sure not call that black fire muscle
  no invisible psychic dungeon
no gentle vision strait jacket, lets call that peoples army, or
  wapendtizi or
    simba
wachanga, but we not gon call it jesus, and not gon worship
  jesus, throw
jesus out yr mind. Build the new world out of reality, and new
  vision
we come to find out what there is of the world
to understand what there is here in the world!
to visualize change, and force it.
we worship revolution

A New Reality Is Better Than a New Movie!

How will it go, crumbling earthquake, towering inferno,
juggernaut, volcano, smashup, in reality, other than the
feverish nearreal fantasy of the capitalist flunky film hacks
tho they sense its reality breathing a quake inferno scar on
their throat even snorts of 100% pure cocaine cant cancel
the cold cut of impending death to this society. On all
the screens of america, the joint blows up every hour and
a half for two dollars an fifty cents. They have taken the
niggers out to lunch, for a minute, made us partners nigger
Charlie) or surrogates (boss nigger) for their horror. But
just as superafrikan mobutu cannot leopardskinhat his way
out of responsibility for lumumba's death, nor even with his
incredible billions rockefeller cannot even save his pale ho's
titties in the crushing weight of things as they really are. How
will it go, does it reach you, getting up, sitting on the side of the
bed, getting ready to go to work. Hypnotized by the machine,
and the cement floor, the jungle treachery of trying to survive
with no money in a money world, of making the boss 100,000
for every 200 dollars you get, and then having his brother get
you for the rent, and if you want to buy the car you helped
build, your downpayment paid for it, the rest goes to buy his
old lady a foam rubber rhinestone set of boobies for special
occasions when kissinger drunkenly fumbles with her blouse,
forgetting himself.

If you don't like it, what you gonna do about it. That was the
question we asked each other, & still right regularly need to
ask. You don't like it? Whatcha gonna do, about it?? The real
terror of nature is humanity enraged, the true technicolor
spectacle that hollywood cant record. They cant even show
you how you look when you go to work, or when you come
back. They cant even show you thinking or demanding the
new socialist reality, its the ultimate tidal wave. When all
over the planet, men and women, with heat in their hands,
demand that society be planned to include the lives and
self determination of all the people ever to live. That is the
scalding scenario with a cast of just under two billion that they
dare not even whisper. Its called, "We Want It All . . .

   The Whole World!"

A Poem for Deep Thinkers

Skymen coming down out the clouds land
and then walking into society try to find out
whats happening—"Whats happening," they be saying
look at it, where they been, dabbling in mist, appearing &
disappearing, now there's a real world breathing—inhaling
exhaling concrete & sand, and they want to know what's
happening. What's happening is life itself "onward & upward,"
the spirals of fireconflict clash of opposing forces, the
  dialogue of
yes and no, showed itself in stabbed children in the hallways of
schools, old men strangling bankguards, a hard puertorican
  inmate's tears
exchanging goodbyes in the prison doorway, armies sweeping
wave after wave to contest the ancient rule of the minority. What
draws them down, their blood entangled with humans,
their memories, perhaps, of the earth, and what they thought it
could be. But blinded by sun, and their own images of things,
rather than things as they actually are, they wobble, they
stumble, sometimes, and people they be cheering alot, cause
they think the skymen dancing, "Yeh . . . Yeh . . . get on
it. . . . ," people grinning and feeling good cause the skymen
dancing, and the skymen stumbling, till they get the sun out
they eyes, and integrate the inhead movie show, with the

material reality that exists with and without them. There are
tragedies, tho, a buncha skies bought the loopdieloop program
from the elegant babble of the ancient minorities. Which is
where they loopdieloop in the sky right on just loopdieloop
in fantastic meaningless curlicues which delight the thin gallery
owners who wave at them on their way to getting stabbed in the
front seats of their silver alfa romeos by lumpen they have gotten
passionate with. And the loopdieloopers go on, sometimes
spelling out complex primitive slogans and shooting symbolic
smoke out their gills in honor of something dead. And then
they'll make daring dives right down toward the
earth and skag cocaine money whiteout and crunch iced into
the statue graveyard where Ralph
Ellison sits biting his banjo
strings retightening his instrument for the millionth time before
playing the star spangled banjo. Or else loopdieloop loopdieloop
up higher and higher and thinner and thinner and finer
refiner, sugarladdies in the last days of the locust, sucking
     they greek lolliepops.
Such intellectuals as we is baby, we need to deal in the real
world, and be be in the real world. We need to use, to use, all
the all the skills all the spills and thrills that we conjure, that we
construct, that we lay out and put together, to create life as
beautiful as we thought it could be, as we dreamed it could be,
as we desired it to be, as we knew it could be, before we took
off, before we split for the sky side, not to settle for endless
meaningless circles of celebration of this madness, this madness,
not to settle for this madness this madness madness, these yoyos
yoyos of the ancient minorities. Its all for real, everythings for
real, be for real, song of the skytribe walking the earth, faint
smiles to open roars of joy, meet you on the battlefield they say,
they be humming, hop, then stride, faint smile to roars of open

joy, hey my man, what's happening, meet you on the
    battlefield
they say, meet you on the battlefield they say, what i guess needs
    to be discussed here tonight
is what side yall gon be on

POETRY FOR THE ADVANCED
1979

Pres Spoke in a Language

Pres

      spoke in a language
"of his own." What did he say, between the
horn line
s, pork pie hat
tenor tilted
pres once was a drummer but gave it up cause other dudes
    was getting
the foxes
while he packed his tomtoms
"Ding Dong," pres sd, meaning
like a typewriter, its the end
of this
line. "No Eyes," pres wd say, meaning
I didn't cdn't dig it, and what it was was
lame. Pres
had a language
and a life, like,
all his own,
but in the teeming whole of us he lived
toooting on his sideways horn
translating frankie trumbauer into
Bird's feathers
Tranes sinewy tracks

the slickster walking through the crowd
surviving on a terrifying wit
its the jungle the jungle the jungle
we living in
and cats like pres cd make it because they were clear they, at
    least,
had to,
to do anything else.
Save all that comrades, we need it.

REGGAE OR NOT!
1981

Reggae or Not!

A piece to be read with Reggae accompaniment.

Inside beyond our craziness is reality. People rushing through life
dripping with
funk. Inside beyond our craziness and the lies of philistines
who never wanted to be anything
but Bootsie
w/ golden curls
and a dress tho they black as tar
beyond our inside, beyond wvo, beyond craziness
dripping with
reality
is the funk
the real fusion of life and life
heart and history
color and motion grim what have you's
beat us eat us send us into flight
on the bottom-ism on the bottom
up under-ism, up under
way down-ism way down under-ville
feet bottoms, everybody put us down
we down
how we got down
how we got, hot, how we got so black
& blue
how we cd blow

how we cd know
how we cd, and did, and is, and bees, how
how how, and how how how, and how and why and why why
like big eye nigger motion
heavywt champ
white hope party
populists in hoods
the real jesse jackson
our history
our pain
our flight
our fright
our terror . . . AHEEESSSSHHHHHHHHEEEEEEEEEEEEEEEEEEE
our women watched when the crackers cut off our balls
in the grass, they made the little girls watch
stuffed them in our mouths
(this was before they complained about
OPEC, before they complained about baraka being rude
before malcolm set kenneth clark on fire
(and after too . . .

        but history
          the development of the afroamerican nation
        in the black belt south.

from blue slaves
from green africa
from drum past and pyramid hipness
from colors colors all the time, everyday, bright—bright—brightness
    red green yellow purple orange wearing niggersssss
        AAAAAAHHHHHH
    violet violent shiny head shiny shoe knife carryin niggersssssss
          AAAAAAAAA
           dust, cripples staggering

white hats, blood, blood in the cotton
wear the fuck out it
love you baby
drunk motherfucker
preachin in the twilight madness and jesus fuckem
hell all around
white face hell
inside beyond the madness history
beyond the scag, history
beyond the oppression and exploitation
Aheeeeeeeeeeee—balls
in the sand
preach!!
baldhead rip off
teach!!
chicken eatin metaphysical
loud talkin chained up motherfuckas
anykinda nigger jet plane flyin ishmael reed lyin nigger
andy young hung like a sign announcing the new policy
get a paycheck pay the madness pay the blood pay the history
beyond the sick ness and racism
history
today's combustion
for the revolutionary future
beyond the madness and cocaine
beyond the male chauvinism and baby actin niggers
who want disco to substitute for their humanity &
struggle
And the alligators clappin they hands Garvey, man
yeh, Nat man, alligators in the sunlight
in the day time now
sittin beside us groundin
man, I see it

it no fool I
I no be fool dem tink
no fool I
alligators Marcus
Nat man, they come right up to us
and explain scientific why our shit aint right
why we need to be under dem,
why we need to bend and sway like
dead boy wilkie, downtown with them
no fool I, I no for fool, bee, bee crazy sometime
sometime be out, be way out,
like crazy mother fucka
purple language come out I mouth
ya know,
but Nat man,
Marcus,
alligator
they organize to love us
take us out ourselves
got whip mout whip eye whip talk
all for fool I but I no be no fool for they
I no go for ghost, like dig, pig, I fuck you up for fun

like a dance
like pussy russo in the joint
want to control the pills
instead the blood drove a shank in his titty
ya punk he scream they take him into solitary
an alligator
he say why you want to separate bozo
((that he inside name for I
bozo, like H.Box Brown say, the muthafucka
upsidedown

186

he bozo
    I—I
           all eyes, a we eye, us, like raging black purpleness
        as music, as rhythmic sun screams our color lay
          for them
The nation, he said,
he had been cut,
the nation
does not, he said,

          and before he cd get it out
          I drove the blade deep down thru
          the adam's apple, severing the jugular

          and man, hey, instead a blood
          ya know, the racist punk,
          all words spill out
           all words run on ground like bleach waterbug
         all words say no, like lula, say no, say, like
           lula, no
       say, hey, say, no, like lula, trying to kill i i no like clay
      say he, words spill out where blood shd be, abstract
        shit all out
     say hey, why you gonna split

         1979 a calm time compared
        1979 cool compared to what will be
      1979 fire in me banked compared
     up against what will be
all I's we, this cant go on
this cant go on, all this
this craziness, beyond it is us
     is history, our lives, and
     the future. Beyond this

beyond craziness, beyond capitalism
beyond national oppression and racism
beyond the subjugation of women
disco bandit style beyond
lies of the disco bandit
beyond lies of the mozart freaks
beyond joe papap and papap joe
beyond breznev, and all the little multi-colored
    breznev clones
    masquerading as radicals telling persons they
    revolutionaries
  beyond all the little latest generation of human failure
    pettybourgeois
 explainers of the bullshit, beyond everything but what will
  last what is
real, what the people will make and demand, what they are
  and have been,
there is Self Determination and Revolution
There is Revolution and Self Determination
there is the fire so broad a rainbow of fire, a world full of fire
there is all bullshit for now exploding
so ready all busshit for next be explode
all fire so flame rise so for fire be heavy and everywhere now

Self Determination
& Revolution
Revolution
& Self Determination
       (sing)

World, to be, for I and that person
and every person, for all I's all we's all they's all all's together be
cool now compared to explosion life future
when every minute is blow up of everyting stupid always
is cool now compared to all exploded jack the ripper rich ass
to people smashed powerful garbage dead forever by our hand

to destroyed dumb systems of exploited pain corrected by
    annihilation only
forever till the next shit
be in the struggle conscious comrade
be in the struggle righteous friend
its cool now, the nation, the workers mad but shit aint rose
beyond the calmness history and pain
beyond the torture history and future fill each other with flame
its cool now, the alligators talking to us like we cant see whats
    on they mind
jimmy carter cant talk to you
jesse jackson cant talk to you
bootsie and the funkadelic cant talk to you
Who can talk to you—who can still bullshit you
                who can set you up with lies you aint heard
                    with unscientific science and metaphysical analysis
            alligators in the disguise of the hiptime
        alligators from the old alligator pad,
        fake communists, sham revolutionaries
        they can and do and will till broke head screams
        talk to you they can shorenuff anyway busshit the besta
    you, but a alligator got bad breaff smell like a alligator
    a alligator eyes is white and bloodshot, full of alligator
    images, a alligator brain is fulla alligator thoughts teethy
    and slimy and fulla dead half ate animals, a alligator bite
    when they talk and they tryin to con you they be bitin
        and it
        hurt so you bash them and they look at you weird you
            say stop
        bitin muthafucka and talk if you goin to i dont eat no
            alligator
        but they make hip pouches to carry my goddam papers in
It's a higher level of bullshit goin down

a much higher level of bullshit
goin down, aint even bullshit, its alligator shit
some sophisticated amphibian feces goin down
up under they bumps and tears, up under they alligator eyes
mostly up under they alligator
lies. a much higher level of bullshit goin down

do you really think Henry Winston was hipper than Rochester
    and if so why
do you really think Andy Young was hipper than Andy Old
or that Angela Davis was hipper than Beaulah or Poncho be
    with Cisco
or that Alligators got sidekicks hipper than Gabby was with
    Roy & Dale
Some sidekick muthafuckers some sidekicks, want us to call
    the nation sidekickania
got sidekick inside they eyes eat and breathe love bein
    sidekicks and got sidekickitis
so much grey stuff hang out they ears droolin eye tears into dirt
come out the closet sidekicks
its calm now & cool, 1979 a calm time, sidekicks can still get over
ride alligators upriver to trade, the jungle is smokin but coolin
and the sidekick deals get made. Come out the closet sidekick
Roy Rogers retired, Cisco doin reruns
Mantan been canonized by the Sidekick society
And Booker T. been made an official militant on the lower
    east side

cant tell multinational unity
from side kick-ism-itis might even fight us
but all folk got to dig it for be real
for be hot
for be us
for be life thrown into future

too much pain go down
too much hate
too many people like we, no go for alligator
                                        ghost
        we is nation in suffering
        we is nation in chains
        the latest spears will not even be spears
        tho the warcries sound the same
        reach out for the comrades reach out for true comrades
        reach out for allies reach out for real allies
        no fool I this alligator, all I's look for light
        we no be fool for alligator, nor the alligator big time friend
        We be for heat & fire
        We be for genuine war
        No be fool for alligator
        Self Determination ⎫
                              ⎬ (sing)
        Revolution   ⎭
        We know our friend for fighting
        We know our comrade for struggle
        no be bullshit only for word noise
        no be dry dull stuff but war war war war war
        fuck a bourgeois alligator
        lyin he tryin to be help
        we know our friend for fighting
        we see our comrade they struggle
        no be fool for alligator
        with some new time chauvinistic lie, by, by, by, no fool I
                                        by, no fool all I

dead folks dead pass away
rich shit dead pass away
liars imitating revolution die
pass away
beyond bullshit is history

beyond deadshit is history & pain
niggers riding alligators will get blown away when the alligator do
even in the calmest of times
Self Determination Revolution
Revolution Self Determination } (sing)
We no be fool
for alligator
our comrade hear and understand
To liberate we got kill
To liberate blood must flow
To liberate imperialism gotta go
we for kill racism, we for kill our oppression and every other person
too
alligator bullshit for big time rich folks
he bite yr militance off like sleepy monkey with tail
in the wrong place
its calm now, jojo, story teller, compared to other future time hotting
hotting be back be back be black be black and all other color too
we for win anyway
we for all us win
we in people laughing our victory song
our victory
song go like this

Self Determination
Revolution
Self Determination
Revolution
Self Determination 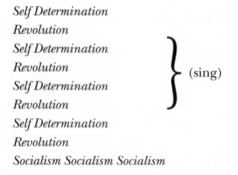 (sing)
Revolution
Self Determination
Revolution
Socialism Socialism Socialism

DEATH TO ALLIGATOR EATING CAPITALISM
DEATH TO BIG TEETH BLOOD DRIPPING IMPERIALISM
I be black angry communist
I be part of rising black nation
I be together with all fighters who fight imperialism
I be together in a party with warmakers for the people
I be black and african and still contemporary marxist warrior
I be connected to people by blood and history and pain and struggle
We be together as party as one fist and voice
We be I be We, We We, the whole fist and invincible flame
We be a party soon, we know our comrade for struggle
We be war to come we bring war we no go for alligator
we kill his trainer too

Self Determination
Revolution
Self Determination } (sing)
Revolution
Socialism Socialism Socialism

Only Socialism will save
the Black Nation
Only Socialism
will save the Black Nation
Only Socialism will save
America
Only Socialism will save
the world!

AM/TRAK
1979

1

Trane,
Trane,
History Love Scream Oh
Trane, Oh
Trane, Oh
Scream History Love
Trane

2

Begin on by a Philly night club
or the basement of a cullut chuhch
walk the bars my man for pay
honk the night lust of money
oh
blow —
scream history love

Rabbit, Cleanhead, Diz
Big Maybelle, Trees in the shining night forest
Oh
blow
love, history

Alcohol we submit to thee
3x's consume our lives
our livers quiver under yr poison hits
eyes roll back in stupidness
The navy, the lord, niggers,
the streets
all converge a shitty symphony
of screams
    to come
    dazzled invective
Honk Honk Honk, "I am here
to love
it". Let me be fire-mystery
air feeder beauty"
Honk
Oh
scream—Miles
comes.

   3

Hip band alright
sum up life in the slick
street part of the
world, oh,
blow,
If you cd
nigger
man

Miles wd stand back and negative check
oh, he dug him—Trane
But Trane clawed at the limits of cool

slandered sanity
with his tryin to be born
raging
shit
     Oh
     blow,
          yeh go do it
          honk, scream
          uhuh yeh—history
               love
               blue clipped moments
               of intense feeling.
"Trane you blows too long".
Screaming niggers drop out yr solos
Bohemian nights, the "heavyweight champ"
smacked him
   in the face
his eyes sagged like a spent
dick, hot vowels escaped the metal clone of his soul
fucking saxophone
tell us shit tell us tell us!

   4

There was nothing left to do but
be where monk cd find him
that crazy
mother fucker
       duh duh-duh duh-duh duh
       duh duh
       duh duh-duh duh-duh duh
       duh duh
       duh duh-duh duh-duh duh

            duh duh
            duh Duuuuuuuuuuhhhhhh
Can you play this shit? (Life asks
Come by and listen

& at the 5 Spot Bach, Mulatto ass Beethoven
& even Duke, who has given America its hip tongue
checked
checked
Trane stood and dug
Crazy Monk's shit
Street gospel intellectual mystical survival codes
Intellectual street gospel funk modes
Tink a ling put downs of dumb shit
pink pink a cool bam groove note air breath
a why I'm here
a why I aint
& who is you - ha - you - ha - you - ha
Monk's shit
Blue Cooper 5 Spot
was the world busting
on piano bass drums & tenor

This was Coltrane's College. A Ph motherfuckin d
sitting at the feet, elbows
& funny grin
Of Master T Sphere
      too cool to be a genius
he was instead
Theolonius
with Comrades Shadow
on tubs, lyric Wilbur
who hipped us to electric futures
& the monster with the horn.

5

From the endless sessions
money lord hovers oer us
capitalism beats our ass
dope & juice wont change it
Trane, blow, oh scream
yeh, anyway.

There then came down in the ugly streets of us
inside the head & tongue
of us
a man
black blower of the now
The vectors from all sources—slavery, renaissance
bop charlie parker,
nigger absolute super-sane screams against reality
course through him
AS SOUND!
    "Yes, it says
this is now in you screaming
recognize the truth
recognize reality
& even check me (Trane)
who blows it
Yes it says
Yes &
Yes again   Convulsive multi orgasmic
                   Art
                   Protest

& finally, brother, you took you were
    (are we gathered to dig this?

electric wind find us finally
on red records of the history of ourselves)

The cadre came together
the inimitable 4 who blew the pulse of then, exact
The flame the confusion the love of
whatever the fuck there was
      to love
Yes it says
blow, oh honk-scream (bahhhhhhh—wheeeeeeee)

(If Don Lee thinks I am imitating him in this poem,
this is only payback for his imitating me—we
are brothers, even if he is a backward cultural nationalist
motherfucker—Hey man only socialism brought by revolution
can win)

              Trane was the spirit of the 60's
              He was Malcolm X in New Super Bop Fire
              Baaahhhhh
              Wheeeeeee . . . Black Art! ! !
Love
History
   On The Bar Tops of Philly
in the Monkish College of *Express*
in the cool Grottoes of Miles Davis Funnytimery
Be
Be
Be reality
Be reality alive in motion in flame to change (You Knew It!)
                       to change!!
          (All you reactionaries listening
          Fuck you, Kill you
          get outta here! ! !)

Jimmy Garrison, bass, McCoy Tyner, piano, Captain Marvel Elvin
on drums, the number itself—the precise saying
all of it in it afire aflame talking saying being doing meaning
Meditations,
Expressions
A Love Supreme
(I lay in solitary confinement, July 67
    Tanks rolling thru Newark
    & whistled all I knew of Trane
    my knowledge heartbeat
    & he was *dead*
they
said.
And yet last night I played *Meditations*
& it told me what to do
Live, you crazy mother
fucker!
    Live!
    & organize
    yr shit
    as rightly
    burning!

IN THE TRADITION
1982

IN THE TRADITION

for Black Arthur Blythe

"Not a White Shadow
But Black People
Will be Victorious . . ."

Blues walk weeps ragtime
Painting slavery
women laid around
working feverishly for slavemaster romeos
as if in ragtime they spill
their origins like chillers   (lost chillen
in the streets to be
telephoned to by Huggie
Bear from channel 7, for the White Shadow
gives advice on how to hold our homes
together, tambien tu, Chicago Hermano)

> genius bennygoodman headmaster
> philanthropist
> romeos—
> but must coach
> cannot shoot—

> hey coah-ch
> hey coah-ch
> trembling fate wrapped in flags
> hey coah-ch
> you can hug this
> while you at it
> coah-ch

Women become
goils gals grinning in the face of his
no light
Men become
boys & slimy roosters crowing negros
in love with dressed up pimp stupidity death
hey coah-ch
wanna outlaw the dunk, cannot deal with skyman darrell
or double dippin hip doctors deadly in flight
cannot deal with Magic or Kareem . . . hey coah-ch coah-ch
bench yrself in the garbagecan of history o new imperial dog
denying with lying images
our strength & African
funky beauty

      nomatter the three networks idiot chatter

           Arthur Blythe
              Says
                it!
          in the
          tradition

                2

           Tradition
           of Douglass
           of David Walker
           Garnett
           Turner
           Tubman
           of ragers yeh
              ragers

(of Kings, & Counts, & Dukes
of Satchelmouths & SunRa's
of Bessies & Billies & Sassys
& Ma's
Musical screaming
Niggers
yeh
tradition
of Brown Welles
& Brown Sterling
& Brown Clifford
of H Rap & H Box

Black baltimore sister blues antislavery singers
countless funky blind folks
& oneleg country beboppers
bottleneck in the guitarneck dudes
whispering thrashing cakewalking raging
ladies
& gents
getdown folks, elegant as
skywriting
tradition
of DuBois
Baby Dodds & Lovie
Austin, Sojourner
I thought I heard Buddy Bolden

say, you're terrible
you're awful, Lester
why do you want to be
the president of all this
of the blues and slow sideways
horn. tradition of blue presidents

         locked up in the brig for wearing zoot suit
      army pants. tradition of monks & outside dudes
of marylous and notes hung vibrating blue just beyond just after
just before just faster just slowly twilight crazier than europe or its
racist children

            bee-doo dee doop bee-doo dee dooo doop (Arthur
            tradition
            of shooters
            & silver fast dribblers
            of real fancy motherfuckers
            fancy as birds flight, sunward/high
                    highhigh
                    sunward
                    arcs/swoops/spirals
         in the tradition
¼ notes
eighth notes
16th notes
32nds, 64ths, 128ths, silver blue
presidents
            of Langston & Langston Manifestos
            Tell us again about the negro artist
            & the racial mountain so we will not
            be negro artists, Mckay Banjoes and
            Homes In Harlem, Blue Black Boys &
            Little Richard Wrights, Tradition of
For My People Margaret Walker & David Walker & Jr Walker
& Walker Smith Sweet Ray Leonard Rockin in Rhythm w/
   Musical Dukes,
What is this tradition Basied on, we Blue Black Wards
   strugglin
against a Big White Fog, Africa people, our fingerprints are
   everywhere

on you america, our fingerprints are everywhere, Cesaire told
    you
that, our family strewn around the world has made more parts of
    that world
blue and funky, cooler, flashier, hotter, afro-cuban james
    brownier
                a wide panafrican
                world

        Tho we are afro-americans, african americans
let the geographic history of our flaming hatchet motion
                            hot ax motion
                            hammer & hatchet

            our cotton history
            our rum & indigo
                    sugar cane
                    history

Yet, in a casual gesture, if its talk you want, we can say
Cesaire, Damas, Depestre, Romain, Guillen
You want Shaka, Askia, (& Roland Snellings too)
            Mandingo, Nzinga, you want us to drop
            Cleopatra on you or Hannibal
            What are you masochists
                paper iron chemistry
                & smelting
                I aint even mentioned
                    Troussaint or Dessaline
                    or Robeson or Ngugi

Hah, you bloody & dazed, screaming at me to stop yet,
NO, hah, you think its over, tradition song, tradition

211

poem, poem for us together, poem for arthur blythe
   who told us again, in the tradition
              in the
            tradition of

     life & dying
    in the tradition of those klanned & chained
  & lynched and shockleyed and naacped and ralph bunched

hah, you rise a little I mention we also the tradition of amos
   and andy
hypnotized selling us out vernons and hooks and other nigger
   crooks of
gibsons and crouches and other assorted louses of niggers that
   turn from
gold to shit proving dialectics muhammad ali style
But just as you rise up to gloat I scream COLTRANE! STEVIE
   WONDER!
          MALCOLM X!
          ALBERT AYLER!
          THE BLACK ARTS!

Shit & whistling out of my nkrumah, cabral, fanon, sweep—I cry
   Fletcher
Henderson, Cane, What Did I Do To Be So Black & Blue, the
   most perfect
    couplet in the language, I scream Mood Indigo, Black
      Bolshevik, KoKo,
    Now's the Time, Ark of Bones, Lonely Woman, Ghosts, A
      Love Supreme,
    Walkin, Straight No Chaser, In the Tradition
           of life
           & dying
        centuries of beautiful

women

crying

In the tradition

of screamed

ape music

coon hollers

shouts

even more profound

than its gorgeous

sound

In the tradition of

all of us, in an unending everywhere at the same time
line
in motion forever
like the hip Chicago poet Amus Mor
like the Art Ensemble
like Miles's Venus DeMilo

& Horace Silver reminding us

& Art Blakey sending us messages

Black Brown & Beige people

& Pharaoh old and new, Blood Brotherhoods

all over the planet, land songs land poems

land sculptures and paintings, land niggers want still want

will get land
in the tradition of all of us in the positive aspect
all of our positive selves, cut zora neale & me & a buncha other

folks in half. My brothers and sisters in the tradition. Vincent
Smith & Biggers, Color mad dudes, Catlett & White Chas & Wm,

BT, Overstreet
& the 60s muralists. Jake Lawrence & Aaron Douglass & Ademola
Babatunde Building More Stately Mansions
We are the composers, racists & gunbearers
We are the artists
Dont tell me shit about a tradition of deadness & capitulation

of slavemasters sipping tea in the parlor
while we bleed to death in fields
tradition of cc rider
see what you done done
dont tell me shit about the tradition of slavemasters
& henry james I know about it up to my asshole in it
dont tell me shit about bach mozart or even ½ nigger
beethoven
get out of europe
come out of europe if you can
cancel on the english depts this is america
north, this is america
where's yr american music
gwashington won the war
where's yr american culture southernagrarians
   academic aryans
   penwarrens & wilburs
  say something american if you dare
   if you
    can
     where's yr american
     music
      Nigger music?

(Like englishmen talking about *great* britain stop with tongues
 lapped on their cravats you put the irish on em. Say shit
man, you mean irish irish Literature . . . when they say about
 they
you say nay you mean irish irish literature you mean, for the
last century you mean, when you scream say nay, you mean
 yeats,
synge, shaw, wilde, joyce, ocasey, beckett, them is, nay, them is
irish, they's irish, irish as the ira)

you mean nigger music? dont hide in europe—"oh that's
    classical!"
    come to this country
        nigger music?

you better go up in appalachia
and get some mountain some coal mining
songs, you better go down south in our land
& talk to the angloamerican national minority
they can fetch up a song or two, country & western
could save you from looking like saps before the world
otherwise
            Palante!
            Latino, Native American
            Bomba, Plena, Salsa, Rain dance War dance
            Magical invective
            The Latin Tinge
            Cherokee, Sonny Rollins w/Clifford Brown
            Diz & Machito, or Mongo SantaMaria

            Comin Comin World Saxophone Quartet you cannot
stand up against, Hell No I Aint Goin To Afghanistan, Leon
Thomas million year old pygmies you cannot stand up
    against, nor
Black Arthur tellin you like Blue Turhan Bey, Odessa,
    Romance can
Bloom even here in White Racist Land It can Bloom as
    Beautiful,
though flawed by our oppression it can
bloom bloom, in the tradition
                of revolution
                Renaissance
                Negritude

Blackness
Negrissmo
Indigisme
sounding niggers
swahili speaking niggers niggers in turbans
rna & app & aprp & cap black blacks
& assembly line, turpentine, mighty fine female
blacks, and cooks, truck drivers, coal miners
small farmers, iron steel and hospital workers
in the tradition of us
in the tradition of us
the reality not us the narrow fantasy
in the tradition of african american black people/america

nigger music's almost all
you got, and you find it
much too hot

in the tradition thank you arthur for playing & saying
reminding us how deep how old how black how sweet   how
we is and bees
when we remember
when we are our memory as the projection
of what it is evolving
in struggle
in passion and pain
we become our sweet black
selves

once again,
in the tradition
in the african american
tradition
open us

yet bind us
let all that is positive
find
us
   we go into the future
      carrying a world
        of blackness
        yet we have been in the world
        and we have gained all of what there
        is and was, since the highest expression
        of the world, is its total

& the universal
is the entire collection
of particulars

ours is one particular
one tradition
of love and suffering truth over lies
and now we find ourselves in chains
   the tradition says plainly to us fight plainly to us
   fight, that's in it, clearly, we are not meant to be slaves
it is a detour we have gone through and about to come out
in the tradition of gorgeous africa blackness
says to us fight, it's all right, you beautiful
   as night, the tradition
thank you langston/arthur
says sing
says fight
in the tradition, always clarifying, always new and centuries old
says
   Sing!
   Fight!

Sing!
Fight!
    Sing!
    Fight! &c. &c.
        Boosheee dooooo doo
          doooo dee doooo
        dooooooooooo!
        DEATH TO THE KLAN!

HEATHENS

1994

HEATHENS

Freedom Jazz Dance or Dr. Jackle

1   They Ugly
       on purpose!

2   They get high
       off Air Raids!

3   They are the oldest
       continuously functioning
          Serial Killers!

4   They murder
       to Explain
          Themselves!

5   They think
       Humans
          are food.

6   They imitate
       conversation
          by lying

7   They are always naked
       and always dirty

the shower & tuxedo
don't help

8   They go to the bathroom
to have a religious
experience

9   They believe everything is better
Dead. And that everything alive
is their enemy.

10   Plus Heathens is armed
and dangerous.

HEATHENS IN EVOLUTION

When their brains got
large enough
They created
Hell!

HEATHEN BLISS

To be Alive
& Ignorant

DEVIL WORSHIP

is Heathen
Self Respect

CIVIL RIGHTS BILL # 666

The Negro Heathen Enablement Act.

"Essentially, it allows more Negroes to become
Heathens."

HEATHEN TECHNOLOGY & MEDIA

Seek to modernize
cannibalism

& make it
acceptable to

the food.

"CHRIST WAS NEVER IN EUROPE!"

(Kwame Toure)

AT LYNCHINGS
HEATHENS WEAR

WHITE TIE
IN FORMAL
HOOD & ROBE

IN THIS FRENZIED
RITUAL
THEY RECONFIRM
THE SUPERIORITY
OF THEIR CULTURE!

Heathens Think Fascism is Civilization

AND THAT THEY ARE SUPERIOR
TO HUMANS & THAT
HUMANITY IS METAPHYSICAL

To under stand that . . .

can you? I mean really
    really dig what that means . . . It's like monsters roaming the
earth . . . who sting to live, who know no better. Who, like wild
animals, might sing, or make a sound some way, that might
pretend, imitate, a human cry, the sweet rationality of love.

That is the art of it, that it exists and carries with it, so many
complexities, even that craziness, but then aesthetics is
connected to the real. The deadliness of that

ugliness, or uncomprehended smoothness. The technology
of predatory creatures who feed on flesh, who shit on the
tender aspirations of human evolution, because they have no

conception of humanity. Except as that natural yelp, which they can see as somehow, a reflex of what that might be. It took that kind of vision for them to understand the use of religion in the changing world. To cloak themselves in the modest trappings of early christianity, having murdered its prophet for power and profit.

WISE, WHY'S, Y'S
1995

WISE 1

WHY'S (*Nobody Knows
The Trouble I Seen*)
Trad.

If you ever find
yourself, some where
lost and surrounded
by enemies
who won't let you
speak in your own language
who destroy your statues
& instruments, who ban
your omm bomm ba boom
then you are in trouble
deep trouble
they ban your
omm boom ba boom
you in deep deep
trouble

humph!

probably take you several hundred years
to get
out!

WISE 2

Billie's Bounce
Charlie Parker

I was of people
caught in deep trouble
like I scribe you
some deep trouble, where
enemies had took us
surrounded us / in they
country
then banned our
ommboom ba boom

the confusion
the sickness

  /What vision in the blackness
        of queens
        of kings
              /What vision in the blackness
          that head
        & heart
        of yours

      that sweet verse
      you made, I still hear

that song, son
   of the son's son's son's
            son
I still hear that
   song,
   that cry
   cries
   screams
life exploded

   our world exploding us
   transformed to niggers

What vision
in the blackness
your own hand sold you
"I am not a king or queen," your own hand
if you bee of the royal catch
or the tribes soulwarped by the ghoulishness

I still hear those songs and cries
of the sons and sons and daughters and daughters
I still bear that weeping in my heart
that bleeding in my memory

And I am not a king
nor trader in flesh
I was
of the sufferers
I am among those
to be avenged!

WISE 3

Hipnosis
Grachan Moncur III

Son singin
fount some
words/ Son
singin
in that other
language
talkin bout "bay
bee, why you
leave me
here," talkin bout
"up unner de sun
cotton in my hand." Son
singing, think he bad
cause he
can speak
they language, talkin bout
"dark was the night
the ocean deep
white eyes cut through me
made me weep."

Son singin
fount some words. Think
he bad. Speak

they
language.
'sawright
I say
'sawright
wit me
look like
yeh, we gon be here
a taste

WISE 4

Dewey's Circle
David Murray

No coat has I got
no extra chop
no soft bed or favor
no connection with the slaver

dark was the night
our eyes had not met
I fastened my life to me
and tried to find my way

talk did I hear
of fires and burning
and death to the gods

on the dirt where I slept
such talk
warmed me

such talk
lit my way

I has never got nothing but hard times and punishment
Any joy I had I made myself, and the dark woman
who took my hand and led me to myself

I has never got nothing
but a head full of blood
my scar, my missing teeth.

I has never got nothing but
killer frustration/ yes dark
was the night
cold was the ground

I has never got nothing, and talk
of rebellion
warmed me

Song to me, was the darkness
in which I could stand
my profile melted into the black air
red from the flame of the burning big house

in those crazy dreams I called myself
Coltrane
bathed in a black and red fire
in those crazy moments I called myself
Thelonius
& this was in the 19th century!

Y's 18

Explainin' The Blues (Ma Rainey)
"Georgia Tom" Dorsey

What are
these
words

to
tell
it

all?
       facts
       acts
       Do they have
       their own
       words?

       !Exacts!
   The Scientist in love
      w/precision
  but we need
   this
we must have
  it
the exact real
the concrete

what it is
& that whole
is story

Africa
Slave
mind memory
Birth
A land across
      the ocean
Blue Water
Green world
      Blood
& Stopped Motion

These mismatched slaves
they cooled
readjusted
the black
     forever
the white
     till the debt's
     paid
     (for them to
       become
       as new
       as we
       so they
       become
       the overseers)
this world of
     limits
     twists

& opposing
forces

these elements
of constant
Change

What is yr world
& yr face
yr clock's
   confession

Have you slept w/
      the constitution
      3/5ths of the darkness
      spoke to

refer to the records
thereby
dumb romance
it's lie
for a flag's
      health
a class
stealth
      to cover
      its murder
      its beatings

As a domestic
      bleeding
      a near by
      tragedy.

We cd go to Dred Scott
        for testimony
        Henry Bibb

We cd ask Linda B
        or Henry
        The Box

We cd be drawn into
        eternity
        w/David and his
        Appeal

To speak of all
        we have
        feel!

Only reality
        say
Where we will
        go
It's tethers
Its' chains
Its' sick pricks
        inventing
        crushings
        for our lives
        a decoration
        of horror
they cd define
        & understand
they cd justify
        our deaths
        & torture

they cd be clean
    & taking
    a little

    taste

As the lightning
tried to illuminate
Animal life

Their smiles even
    chill us
    mad poseur
    posing as
    the mad doctor
    who is the original

    American
    Nazi
The southern Himmlers
& Goebbels, baked
    in our dying

What the war
    proposed
        our entrance
        as citizens
        who once had been
        slaves

This 13, 14 & 15 yr numbers
    in the
    lottery

This Freedman's Bureau
this 40 acres

     as grounds for
     identical
     social
     valence
     political
     economic

          (not Sociology & Social Democratic
               political
               Bohemianism)

Revolution, The question
    the answer

What revolution
    cd not be
    destroyed
      bought
    or postponed?

What revolution
    cd not be
      sold out?

All those
   in the real
      world

all those
   that have

actually
    been

The betrayal of Niggers was necessary
   to welcome
      Imperialism!

   That was its condition
    The Killing of
       Nigger
         Democracy

So Spain
   it's decorated
     past
The Philippines, Puerto Rico
       Cuba, the booty

The new era

    amidst our sunlight
     mass laughter
      emancipation
       The Paris
        Commune

The Berlin meeting to divide
   the Dark Places
   Colonial Pie

What the Slave Trade
   Wrought.

That one day the Heathens
wd actually come on the real
side - that they wd take our
hearts as funny valentines

That they wd stick our lives & history

in the toilet bowl
          (toxic
          waste)

& claim our
     past
& future

As the Commune
     smashed
        dead

    The rehearsals
          for Buchenwald
          & Belsen
carried out in the
          American
          South

Unwilling nigger actors
              Heavy
              Minstrels
            this torture Birth
            of the

          Black Nation

The "rule by naked terror"

can not be called
    Fascism

because we
    are
Niggers

& that
is too
famous
for the likes
of us

Fascism
    wd come later
    in Europe
    (naturally)
    & be well advertised

    as an excuse
    for Israeli
    imperialism

HISTORY-WISE #22

Black Mountain Blues
Bessie Smith

"The only
      railroad
            guaranteed
not to break down!"

100 years
      Before
      The Col-
        trane
           The
      real
      sub
      way
            Ms "Moses'" Streamliner
            John Parker's Darker
Sparker
at Night
No light
but a far star
North

&wayoff
Like a whistle or a horn

The black night
fills
our ears

We gon' go
has already

gone

"Choo Choo" is the translation
in somebody else's

Station

#

Whooooooeeee Whooooooeeee
Whooooooooooeoooo Whoooooooooeeoooo Whooooeeeeoooo

is its real
sound

from way up under
the ground

Way
Down

Whoooooweeeee   Whooooeeooooeeooo
Whooooeeeeoooooeeeooo

Thats it real
Sound
Under Ground!

& then sometimes
if the night is cold
& bright

that whistle cries
like all through

that night

that whistle cries
& it moans

Whyyyyyyyyyyyyyyyyyyyyyyyyyyyyyyyyyyyyyyyy'sssssssssss
  Whyyyyyyyyyyyyyyyyyyyyyyyyyyyyyyyyyysssssssssssss
    Whyyyyyyyyyyyyyyyyyyyyyyyyyyyyyyyyyyyyyy
                              &c.

1929: Y YOU ASK? (26)

Chime Blues
FletcherHenderson
(piano solo)

In "The Masque of the Red Death"
near the end
of the ball
a deadly stranger appears.
Not Vincent Price,
Some thing with eyes like numbers
mouth a siren about to wail
Screamed headlines, the dope of the radio.
The party goers freeze
the Butlers and Maids get their notices
they are skeleton walkers, boat feet,
Wings, dark countenanced baritones
Willowy sopranos; the hall
Swept with an actual tide
of Red & Black—The White
is the silence as the Flag Waves.

Did some one say, "The Renaissance
is over?" Or was that the living
Dying wind, reality, or the Rags
of yr future? The living dying wind
adhesive against wet w/ blood top hats
souls w/bullet holes. Ex leapers smashed
against the bankruptcy of bullszit & oppression.

Finally we know, half superiorly,
all these guests
will die of the Plague. The Black Death!
The Red Death! The Plague!

Horror movie statistical murders.
Dead in old houses

& under cars. In chain gang Gulags
& share cropper concentration camps.

Most of us wake up in a crumbling
plague ridden mansion.
Imitation music
Imitation laughter
Imitation people
w/ Imitation Lives-
A nation of minstrels
and ignorant powerful people
plus slave niggers almost as insane
as their
oppressors!

A ritual of Black & Red Caped
Devil Messengers
In the shadow of the casement glass

Our glasses, raised in the air,
are frozen
in a shadow
as wet
as blood!

It begins to snow outside
beyond the dead forest,
inside the naked empty grey cities

The snow is spotted w/ blood.
A madman's signature
is shown on television.

Disease, now, is
continuous!

Stellar Nilotic (29)

You Gotta Have Freedom

Pharoah Sanders

You want to know
how I escaped? (There were bright yellow lights now, and red
flashes.)

Can we talk here? Are we all ex-slaves? (a laughter
ruins the dawn silence, and the birds acknowledge us
with their rap of flutes).

That star, just over the grey green peak (the moonlight
acknowledges us and makes us shadows.) Was how I was led,

A slender black woman, around 23, put out her hand, turning
toward the star. You know how night is, the star was blue and
beautiful. Around it music, we drummed through the forests.

Their ignorance, that country of "Their" and its united snakes
unified in madness, and worship of advantage. You cannot
have aristocracy, except you have slaves.

They teach you that.

- - -

- - -

Yet our going, our breathing, the substance
of our lives, was with us chanting
against whatever was not cool.

This was always, and remains
a foreign land. And we are

undoubtedly, the slaves.

There is some music, that shd come on now.
With space for human drama, there shd be some memory
that leaves you smiling. That is, night and the way/
Her lovely hand, extended. The Star, the star, all night
We loved it
like ourselves.

At the Colonial Y They Are
Aesthetically & Culturally Deprived
(Y's Later) (31)

Maple Leaf Rag
Scott Joplin

SHARK MONSTER Rockefeller
      Codes. Explosion is War.
      For Wha? (The Blood)
         Profits
           of New
Avant disease   come to ya'
What was in the bush / yr society
      smoked
      EATS EATS
        its terror
           White Beast
     alive w/ Harpoons
inside it the bones
of whole nations

Slavery, Concentration
Camps, Plantations
Gas Chambers

The death of Reconstruction was
   the death of the dream
   the death of the reality
   The death of any wd be American
      Democracy!

Bloodless "Jaws" whale shark monster
it kills include cultures
now post McCarthy where
is Grapes of Wrath or I Was

A Fugitive or the truth
of itself? Was Sam Spade
a Communist Sympa
thizer? Or Philip Marlowe?
But even that individual cry
for straight shot Democracy
cd finally find itself banned in darkness
while Robotic Horror pornography makes us
consumers of masturbation and degenerating
values.
      An america where the only academy awards
      go to Ronald Reagan w/ Clarence Pendleton as
      Ben Vereen. "Boogity Boogity" an
      Ellison description of Ellison describing.
      The teeth of imperialism is a chant
      for the dying things needing to die.
      Its poison swelling EAT EAT
      Its cry of terror!

You see (a whispered
    aside)
    even its "humanity"
    (a people of slave holders)
    was a kind
    of minstrelsy

    An unconvincing
    Black Face Act.

Now the flicks are a form of Commerce
           less and less
                of art
     Film innovation was revolutionary
Eisenstein's Red Montage
     With that connection, the tech
nology & casual populist dream

     Equality.
     So much popcorn.
'I'he Jews, Italians, Irish, Poles, & c.
     had first to give up
     being that
to enlarge the baby slave holder
     Fat banker fish
to be its evolved "revolutionary"
     Sleek sea thing
          (Sleek?
     A nigger
     in its teeth
The feed of bulging monsters
so creative they invented
fascism in the black belt
of democracy
So the Black Face, Dixie Land, thin rag, non-"race,"
           Funny hat, Paul Whiteman
           stiff seat, noun baked non swing
           of the "cool," bebop's cover.
           Or for the Shorties & Rodgers
           & Bru's & Becks & the green
           of our dollar - oh man- to
           the "progressive jazz" of glass
           adjectives w/ no where to blow.

Until we get fusion & its con
a cool out of new blues
            turns a chain to a flexible
            rubber unbreakable straw
            for yr elevator colored nouveau,

            to the gallows garden
            of the floating compradors

            where their eggs, like body snatcher
            pods lay hatching way in the middle
            of the air.

            This bend of class
            to the death of itself
            & rebirth in fake neon flames.
Elvis Presley was the FDR of
            the 1950's, the philosophy
            was workable & when the
            Beatles moved in simply slander
            them w/belittling Jesus
            & enlarge the American market.
            Nigger Music became figure
            music. Chocolate death
            Plastic. Instead of rejection-
The Huge monster's mouth
Him/Her's protein digesting skin

            To Europe? To The Past?
            But leave reality to the
                real & the living

By the end of the 19th century
they cd convert the sorrow songs
to Barber Shop
Quartets.

"There Was Something I Wanted to Tell You." (33) Why?

African Lullaby
Babenzele Pygmies,
S. Africa

Revolutionary War
gamed
  sold
    out
      The Tories
still in control
of the culture

English Departments
still
& the money & "culture"
in an "English"
accent.

The Green Mtn Boys
Tom Paine The Bill
of Rights

tried to cut
it

   But then 19th century
   Explosion, Free the
   Slaves, Kill feudal

ism, Give rights
to the Farmer & Worker

the vote to Women

But that got blew
     Hayes-Tilden, Bloody
          Democrats

       Traitor
       Republicans

The Ku Klux Klan
(A murder Gang!)

& that leap, into industrial society
democracy they sd
Got all but Killed
     tho murdered
     many times!

Marx, Engels, Lenin, Stalin, Mao, Ho
         Fidel, Nkrumah
         Martin, Sandino
         & Malcolm X

Have all been
betrayed

All revolutions bear their own
betrayal, & betrayers
The world is complex

its reality materially
simple

It is the dying of the life

the quenching of the spark
the greying of the light
the cold whiteness of the recently
full of flaming inspired intelligent
heart! The dead entrail of our
        collective traditional
        enemy. Animal
        connections. Metaphysics.
        Greed. Anti Science
        lives. Ugly in power
        and uglying up our only
        life.

The rot, the lie, the opposite
will always, if there is ever
that, exist. As life means death
and hot cold. Darkness lights'
closest companion. Its twisted,
        & rises as a spiral. It is No &
Yes, and not It for long.

        Motion, the beat, tender mind
you humans even made music.
        But, our memory anywhere
as humans and beyond, parallel
to everything, is rise is new is
Changed, a glowing peaceful
Musical
World.

What betrays revolution is the need
for revolution. It can not stop in life.
Whoever seeks to freeze the moment is

instantly, & for that instant, *mad!*

We are servants of life in upward
progressive motion. Fanners
of the flame. Resistance is Electric.
Fred sd, its measurable on every
block.

The wd be stoppers of revolution
are its fossil fuel

Winter comes
and Spring

We can sometimes
hear
explosions!

YMCA #35

After The Rain
Trane

We talked all the time
   as spirits we were
    allowed.
      & watched the different
       primates in their turns
      & elegant twists

We caught the rising virus
   like a style of neon
   murders. A calm
   blood washing upward

Between giggles & drunk laughter
   wisdom hit the walls
   & ceiling, windows
    closed if open
     opened if
     closed

It was never quiet
   no familiarities
   were permitted

The good guys sat
   & watched the door

the wizards crawled
      from 14th St to the
         outer crust

      Colors & rain
The well dressed well spoken
      The poverty stricken
         The lonely
         The important
            maniacs

They were singing through their
         noses, & fingers
Everybody was a headline
      A massacre that cd not
be a revelated gorilla

      These were rich people & Heroes
   The stink was not stink, the garbage
      not really garbage. If you cd bend concrete
   & hang like the high tent of drunken rapists
Applause wd rock & roll you in yr dreams

Awards could be coughs
      hands reaching
         poetry of climaxes
            proposed. Crippled

         Weasels I knew
            & sang a song
            for the airplane
               underground

Not to be subjective
    a heart full of dashes
        no opening through backs
        exploding in their
        dreams.

It is not enough to witness, you are
   somewhere anyway
     & you wont sweat.

2

Riding through the valley
    Sundays coldness a hole
       in summer. A red dark ball
      pasted over
      with notes

But picture The Tempts
    Do-walking
       clean among black
      waves

Picture a blinding whiteness
    like Cab Calloway's
      shoes

the nigger computers
    bluely reporting
      ghosts ahead
   who are cannibals

We ponder for the Bop-trillionith
time

The Madness
of the Gods

THE TURN AROUND Y36

The Turn Around
Hank Mobley

Jack Johnson

        was convicted
  of White Slavery!
  He was probably
the only person ever
convicted in this
        country
         of Slavery!

               -Coyt's Son

("ONE MORE TIME")

Humph
T. Sphere Monk

Likewise
in all these years
I only seen one time
Downbeat called somebody
a "racist" from the front cover
& that was LeRoi Jones. Was
the only time.

          -Likewise

LORD HAW HAW (AS PYGMY) #37

All Blues
Miles

We were here

        before

    God

    We

       invented

Him.

    Why?
That's a good/ god damn
    question.

SPEECH
#38 (OR Y WE SAY IT THIS WAY)

Be Bop
Diz

OoBlahDee
Ooolyacoo
Bloomdido
OoBopShabam
Perdido Klackto-
      Veestedene
Salt Peanuts oroonie
      McVouty
        rebop

Ornithology
BaBa Ree Bopp

Ooo Shoobie
      Doobie

& The Sisters
Dooie Blah
&
Dooie Blee

a Kuka mop

Bee Doop Doop
      ie Doo

          pie   -Lemon Drop
      Be Doopie
          Doop Dop

      Squirrel
in The Glass
      Enclosure

      of the essential
      Transbluesency

We dreamt Paradise
      w/you
      Naima

Savoying
Balue Bolivared

in black Night
Indigo

Brownie Red
Hollywood Hi Noon
          Trane Lights

      Salaam Thunder
            electricity trademark

Yr heart
in Repetition

            de Milos

Monk's Shades
        made the tru/man
        of a Hairy
            Square
            symbol
        in faded corniness

Gold Electric
Natural Grace
        like
                Freedom
    Horns
of our
    Description - Desperatenesses'
                Drums

Sharp spectrum Blace
            painted hard light

Lush life romance
        ancient
            trade.

Hideehideehidee hee
ooooohhhhhhhhhh

    Oh Imperial Ghost
        who is no
            Ghost
            & Real

Autumn
I think of you

& the sorrow
of gates

& absences in your soul
        America
    like the dead

        spaces

    like ignorance

    between the

        stars

The Ape said,
"Floogie,
        Lucy, Baby!"

Human light
    in your
        African
                Eyes.

    Travelin Travailing
Majestic
                Life Form

        Scatting

        Boogieing

Cosmos In

Cosmos

Rhythm

Rapping, capping
        hand
     slapping

Black Poet

Chanting

to the 1st fire.

So the King Sold the Farmer #39

Angels & Demons At Play
Sun Ra

The   Ghost

       Ghost

Watch out

       for the Ghost

       Ghost get you

       Ghost

       Watch out
            for the
       Ghost

In bitter darkness screams sharpness as smells
    & Seas black voice
    Wails
    in the death filled
    darkness

Their bodies disease beneath intoxicated floors
A seas shudder afraid its turned
              to Blood

The bodies
  they will, in death's shill
  to Lionel Hampton
Ghost Look out
   for the Ghost

Ghost
  is have us
 chains
  is be with
   dying

   is caught

Sea mad, maniac
    drunken
  Killing sea

        Ghoooooooooost

        Ghoooooooooost

The chains
  & dark
  dark &
   dark, if there was "light"
     it meant
       Ghooost

Rotting family we
 ghost ate
    three

A people flattened chained
    bathed & degraded
       in their own hysterical waste

below
beneath
under neath
deep down
up under
        grave cave pit
       lower & deeper
     weeping miles below
           skyscraper gutters

Blue blood hole into which blueness
is the terror, massacre, torture
   & original western
       holocaust

     Slavery

    We were slaves

     Slaves

     Slaves

Slaves
–
Slaves
–
Slaves

–
　　　We were

Slaves

–

Slaves

–

　　They threw
　　　our lives
　　　a way

Beneath the violent philosophy
　　of primitive
　　　cannibals

　　Primitive
　　Violent
　　Steam driven
　　Cannibals

RR

My Brother

Y THE LINK WILL NOT ALWAYS BE "MISSING" #40

The Wise One
Trane

Think of Slavery
    as
    Educational!

FUNK LORE
1995

J. SAID, "OUR WHOLE UNIVERSE IS GENERATED BY A RHYTHM"

Is Dualism, the shadow inserted
for the northern trip. as the northern
trip. minstrels of the farther land,
the sun, in one place, ourselves, somewhere
else. The Universe
is the rhythm
there is no on looker, no outside
no other than the real, the universe
is rhythm, and whatever is only is as
swinging. All that is is funky, the bubbles
in the monsters brain, are hitting it too,
but the circles look like
swastikas, the square is thus
explained, but the nazis had dances, and even some of the
victims would tell you that.

There is no such thing as "our
universe", only degrees of the swinging, what
does not swing is nothing, and nothing swings
when it wants to. The desire alone is funky
and it is this heat Louis Armstrong scatted in.

What is not funky is psychological, metaphysical
is the religion of squares, pretending no one
is anywhere.

Everything gets hot, it is hot now, nothing cold exists
and cold, is the theoretical line the pretended boundary
where your eye and your hand disappear into desire.

Dualism is a quiet camp near the outer edge of the forest.
there the inmates worship money and violence. They are
learning right now to sing, let us join them for a moment
and listen. Do not laugh, whatever you do.

Masked Angel Costume

THE SAYINGS OF MANTAN MORELAND
Alabama

1   Never let a ghost
    Ketch you
                Never!

2   Avoid Death
        Ghosts
        Always
            be
            there!

3   Dead People
    & Live People
    Should not
    Mix!

4   Ghosts think they
            good lookin
    Never stay to find out!

5   I am mentioned in the credits
            but the ghost
                got the
                    dough!

6   Cemeteries
         Funeral Parlors
         Morgues
         Do not need
         You while
         You
                    alive

7   Never let Mr. Chan
     send you into
     a dark
        room
     by
        your self

8   If the dark get
         Noisy
         Seek
         light
            at
         Once!

9   Few people know
         my whole
             name.
             Nor
     if the name
        they call me
             is
             real.

10 Wait until
  the shooting
  stops
  then
  wait
  for
  witnesses
Leave as soon
  as it is
  safe.

11 I am a chauffeur
  when you see
    me
  But that is
   only
  in the
   movies.

12 I am never really
   laughing
   except
  off
  camera.

13 I made a lot of money
  & made people happy
   It was
   a job
  I accepted rather
   than
   preach
    or
   steal!

14   *Birmingham*
       Birmingham
was where
4 of my daughters
were killed

John Coltrane
composed
Alabama

It was the music
that moved
    my feet

        they never
        failed.

Sounding

A Measure, A Song, A Curse

And so the seasons, they tell us
are more important, than ourselves
flies and starlight, all the little
things. Except ourselves. Should you
want one, a self, any way. Detached
from the Death pile of this, the primitive
distortion, still. Prehistoric monsters
cave logic, uncooked stumblings, witchdoctoristic
shit. If you had a self
     If you was up under all that pile
     If you could still breathe or see
     beneath the assault of ancient deadly lies
     kept alive by the infinite sucking needles
     of rich white craziness, of schizophrenic negro
     craziness, the chauvinism of savages, disease
     for sale, famous rotting items to be eaten or
     smeared in the nose and ears, corpse parts
     to paste on the eyes, vomit music, which is
     quiet and stinks and full of vague balls
     flags made of twilight to wrap around anything
     sensitive until it smothers.

                    (Head smashed through a door
                    splinters jabbed in the neck
                    blood is the number to ask for
                    blind visionaries babbling)

They say everything is more important than a self. The whole group of them. Stashed somewhere between the stars blinking and blue, someone intelligent might find us, very very intelligent. Wizards rattling gourds as your leg is about to drop off. A Muslim appears, A Talmudist, A Christian, A Capitalist economist, the rattling gets stronger and the leg finally drops off gangrenous tootsie roll

No selves, only "eats" and "drinks" and drugs and "fucking". No selves. What about only alone, there is no one else, its OK then, no one can tell. A tree felled in the forest, there's no sound in New York. It doesnt exist then, in Omaha or Heaven. No selves, not together, thinking. Not alive and actually planning in the world to change it. Not no science, no. No selves then, collected, and eyes blinking. None of that. A coffin, lets kill ourselves. Lets get a bomb a big explosive mushroom volcano and drop it on ourselves. No selves, lets blow up everything. Lets blow up men and women and children and thought and feeling. Lets make it flat and burned. Lets be radioactive and write poems about paths in connecticut. About birdbaths in vermont and wisps of smoke in south hampton. no selves, not even one, except alone. an individual is OK, only alone. not with touching and seeing in it. not with no intimate whispering. Keep bullshit like love out of it. none of that. no selves. only 12 hr barbaric killing of niggers and white ass working class motherfuckers with hard hands.

Bees darting. A cloud. Light dancing. Twiddle dee and tweedle doo and silent bumps. no being and stuff. no wanting except gold vinyl spots. you can want gold vinyl spots. No being more, only being less except you can be more if that is less. Or not real. or dies easy. Or full of shit.

Just death. Call it open up and live. Call it mystery man. Music.
Call it hey hey hey eureka the freaka, say, ART! Let it rain fire
but it wont because it cdnt in the birdbath martini fingertip
silences, pages can be turned but have silly shit in em. quiet
death. Cheever in cold. in sides of stuff with no outsides. no
connect. no heat except from furnaces if you got oil. no warm
– no warm – no meaning. Ashes! Ashes! White people Academy
Awards. Ashes! Niggers in dinner jackets! Ashes, Fat nigger with
comments. Niggers with pulitzer prize cover story schizophrenia
is OK. be a indian. be anonymous. but dont be no indian like
brown and off somewhere hurting. be an indian if you aint an
indian. if you really an indian be something else. Ashes. Relics.
Lets be relics, but not too much of a relic. Not way back to black
relics. no black relics. vanished. lied. Stolen. Not like the shit the
pope got hid in his museum. something without blood. without
sweat. without words passing through ears. Ashes.

& no selves. Bombs are cool. Beatniks like bombs. Bombs are
cool. Ashes.

Death. Racism. Lies. Chauvinism. Oppression. Exploitation.
Frustration. White movies. TV with only Nell Carter and the
nigger midget. And Benson. Fake families. Artificial. Be artificial.
Be Oscar Wilde. But dont try to fuck. Be cute. but no fucking.
Stop fucking. Freaky fucking is OK in a newspaper or rolled
up in a window shade. or in a book. No fucking. No babies.
No real shit. No cold except cold as nothing nothing out
there. Ashes. Let bombs fall. Let killing be everything then
nothing. Conan the barbarian. Reagan the Conan. Ashes.
Fighting shd be over, peace. not peace where people are happy.
but peace of death. death peace. peace of death. silence and
ice death ashes. fire is over. traces of fire is OK but no fire in
nothing. no heart of eye fire. no fire for food, except if cooked

by silent nigger, or laughing nigger, or different kinds of
colored darkies who can be called names.

But no selves, hear? No breathing. No dancing. Except if you
bounce. No rhythm. Either be on the wall or off the wall.
But be against people having intelligence without degrees.
No intelligence without degrees. Be for Norman Podhoretz
dream of a world of ashes in which Reagan is crowned Lord
God of Barbarians. Uphold Barbarians. Uphold Tarzan. Be
Boy. Appoint Cheetah as Civil Rights Commissioner.
Uphold blackface but kill black faces. Darkies are great.
Guys who can get along, and Gals. Uphold Gals. Pat em on the
ass if it wiggles. Big ass Gals. And ashes. And bouncing. Be for
bouncing. Bounce. And Death, Be for death. Death from
the skies. Death as a result of barbarian economies. Greed
Death. Stupid Death. Hail to Stupid Death & Bouncing.
Hail to Awkward Dumb shit. And death. And sky death. And
Gestapos and Nazis. Be for preachers who want to burn books.
and Ashes. And bouncing. And death. No selves. No collections
of them. Kill collections of selves. Alone is OK. solipsism.
greed. Individualism. and death. And ashes. And cold sand
instead of warmth, or vibrance or rhythms, or intelligence
loose in the world. Dead art. Art with feathers. Denying Art.
Schizophrenic art. Ruler Art. Museum Art. No artists who want
information or the world in it.

silence any art with the world in it or close to it or talking
or thinking. kill light and heat that is among us. kill us.
there is no us. only blindness and ice ages. no science. no
love. no reason. no family. no communities of intelligence.
no development. no loving human peace. Ashes. Stanley.
Livingston. Sky death. No selves. dumbness. dull poems.
bouncing. assassinations. klan sympathies. and ashes. and

imperialist war. yes, that finally, and everything thing thing thing thing that supports or justifies it. stupid exclusive national chauvinism and ʀᴜ (what))) and sidekicks and ashes and bouncing atomic war thats what we need atomic war we gonna get it theres no we, us i's is gonna, aint no us/es no no no only death and ashes and bouncing, no selves, fuck you kill you niggers, anythings, nothing but atomic death from rich people there is only ashes and bouncing thats all no love no selves no peace only atomic war and death and ashes thats all no no no self no no no no selves no no no no world no no no no no no no

BROTHER OKOT*

1931–1983

Our people say
death lives
    in the West
(Any one
can see
    plainly, each evening
where the sun
goes to die)

      So Okot
      is now in the West

      Here w/ us
      in hell

      I have heard
      his songs
      felt the earth
      drum his
      dance
his wide ness
& Sky self

*Okot P'Bitek, great Ugandan poet

                Ocoli Singer
                Ocoli Fighter
              Brother Okot
        now here w/ us
        in the place

        Where even the Sun
              dies.

FORENSIC REPORT

The Killers cd wear
    spurs
    or
    medals

    Ears
cd be on
    their
    head

They cd be blonde
    & american
    & from the
    South

They cd speak American
    & live
    in Virginia
    or Maine
    or California
    or D.C.

They cd be wealthy
    & have a degree

They cd have little
        children
        who cd also

        be killers
        or have already
        killed

        They cd
        have proof
    that they killed
only out of necessity

They cd be dressed up
        or naked
        or both
        at once

They wd not have
        to laugh
        They could
        not have
        to love any thing

They could look
        perfectly
        normal
            to
        themselves

But be hated
        most places

They would not
      have to
      be seen
      drinking blood.

They wd not have to be known
      widely
      except
   as a metaphor

They wd not have to be sane
      They cd act crazy
      as well

They would not always
      be able
         to
         trick
         people.

      They cd
      be killed
   in the right
      Situation

      IT'S
      NOT NECESSARY
      THAT THEY UNDERSTAND

      THIS.

Why It's Quiet in Some Churches

Just a Closeta Walk with Thee

Not a pin drops. No breathing. Please, please no sound.
("Make them niggers cut out that 'tom foolery'. Jesus,
ain't in Georgia!")
> You cannot make noise or the spirit will hear
> We'll nail up your mouth if you try to sing
> We changed the spelling of Prophet to Profit
> We changed Soul to Sole
> We covered spirit with a ghost
> We changed Sun to Son, and with the help of the right Farther
and knowledge of What Goest? He cd get his rightful
> inheritance.
No. we took the mother out. We burned broads from Salem to
> Troy.
From Soweto to Philadelphia to transform the pyramid of life
to a triangle of death. We took the head and nuts off the ankh
changed the life sign to a cemetery advertisement. Then had mfs
wear death around the necks they wd long for it so. We dis
> connected
creativity and art. But if it ain't no creativity ain't no art, and if ain't
no art even the schools must close, and the schoolmen go back to
Hairy Mystery!
The Father The Son And The Holy Ghost is a Joke
What happened to the Mother, Fools! There is no
life without the mortar and the pestle, the thing and

the thang, without boys and girls, women and men
in their blue quivering funk rising till jism
brings a new day.
We created tragedy by killing our fathers, fucking our mothers
putting out our own eyes, and wandering the world as a
advertisement for "modernism"
We separated thought from feeling. We thought feeling wd stop
us thinking, or vice versa. But then I do want to bore you.
And the cross roads we took recrossed, recrossed, and the
cold north
was not that any more, but we were anyway, and then to exist
was only possible
w/ the slandered smoke of tortured change. From its we
became ex-its!
We were signs but w/o the seed, blind, we had egos instead of
eggs
the missing excitement, Gee, Baby, Sin! Our epitaph!

Sin Soars!

The American Peoples' Voice
    is never heard well
    is seldom heard
ABC CBS NBC Rocky Dupont Mellon Rich
    Thieves & Murderers is
    Pretend human real animals
    is Animal's that own network, newspaper
    chains, IBM, & them. Krupp
    & Dutch Phillips, the Japanese & German
    corporations, Israeli Bankers &
    the private collectors of the debt
    of any nation
    They
    Is
    Not But Not
     the American
      people
their voice is never
       well seldom
       heard
English Department Skull & Crossbone
      New Critic Klansman is
      deconstructing the day
      name for night slaughter
      They laugh, They soul they do not have

The American people voice
        Eurocentric Cultists
        of white supremacy own it
        they own the super structure
        for the business of planets
        shit namers
        we call them
        they name shit
        & get us to buy
        shit & eat shit
they voice is
they voice, is always,
                is
                heard

        But Not the American People
            not many people
            real people
            whole people

        Not Americans of any Kind – Definitely not
Native Americans or African Americans
                            Puerto Rican
                            or Chicano
                Americans
                            Central Americans
                            South Americans
        Invaders of Panama is
        us/ussr Con artists ripping off Nicaragua
        is, always is, Contras, Klan,
        Nazis is, Seldom the people
                is
        The downside negative

But not the American people
the corporations censor the American
peoples' voice.
                        People who own
radio stations
                    People who own
        tv networks
                        They can be heard
                        Chicken Kings
                        Hotel Queens

                        But not the American
people
        The American People
        Their voice
is never
        heard

So now they voices we hear are selling us
They voices carried in image profane
The voices & images jarring our favorite
        movies in shatters
            of sell

Like the German & Japanese Economies
They return via Dark Shadows
to Gold Light Hoorays
Gold   Flood   Sun   Burst
            Hoo
            Rays
They sell CBS records & CBS
films, Miles & Monk & Billie
& Duke belong to Samarai, Inc.
Frank Capra, Orson Welles, Sidney

Poitier, Rita Hayworth, belong
now to Samurai, Inc, a sub sidiary division of Standard
Oil of New York
> Gimme a s
> Gimme a o
> Gimme a N
> Gimme a Y

> S O N Y   S O N Y
Standard Oil of New York

So they transfered control of German
& Japanese corporations at the end of
World War 2 to Rocky's holdings
Through Farben & Mitsubishi the good S
went on

With Marshall & his plan they lifted
the spoils, w/ our deaths & our toils
& gave them legally to themselves
While Truman lied & Eisen
hower choked on the oat meal.

They gave themselves money to defend
our wealth in their pockets as
security guards of Samurai, Inc.
As Samurai, Inc as Allah u
Akbar oil Gods, Inc., as legislators
governors, as money- & murder-dents
as any & every as what it is
was & their will over done

to the bone
to the minstrel grin
to the marrow of electrocution
to the splinters of serial kill
to the tap dances of thugs

       They cough up nothing but Germs
       In the ditch of history
       they lie
       They old & wiggle in ice cubes knocking
       Cold non rhythm jolt of
       Swastika
       the sauerkraut of
       vulture grease
       the hot dogs with
       black catch/up
       yellow retard
       omnipotent Frauds
       bounced help
   the money crosses water as dots
   & dashes smelling nothing
   the sos is you breathing
   crossing the death row of
   Rockefeller's day dreaming teeth

they have sold our future to themselves
disguised as foreign languages
& dusty ledgers
the legs are sprawled so the dirty boots
elaborate the stillness
the letters awry
the tolls cooking us
the oil lamps of

brokeness
ghetto ness
Barrio Azul we
    clack
    maracas
    of the pulse
    the awaiting
as delusion cops a feel

Our map is not at all
    What it need &
        would be
          if we

    but then   our map
        is sliced out
        with the newspaper
        with the Morality
          of pay toilets
          & where we are
          is old business
      the blurred memory
          of certain
          arthritic dips

So why are we, the unheard, the ones
for whom democracy is a republican
        pornograph
        needing only a sharp slave
        to play
we the why do we who are burning
      our flags
      with the cocaine

of them guys
the propaganda fist
of green backs
we who no have
no see
no know
Why do we
Who are not with one person
or
one vote
who went to electoral
college
to study
Dip Craft
Fraud Light
Who do not remember the 3 Musketeers
Who do not admit to being Dartagnan
Yet are
from 1 second past
monkey

why do we who are not heard
the American people
why do we not dig
How come
we dont under
stand
That the US is Japan & Germany now
That Russia & China are the new Colored
Guys
& the niggers are making all
the trouble
it's the niggers
even they

it's said
are somewhere
making trouble
& they doing, it's said, also
A good f - - - - - g
job
cause thats all
we
not
knowing
got

what news? no voice
for the criminal
class

you're just in time
not to be.

No voice, insist our
Not
Masters
the snake is
rolling
cross
the
ground
Our saviour rolls across the clouds
in Air Force One   Is our voice
riding high w/ him?
Heading for Panama, Nicaragua, Grenada

Now breathing vampire blood mixed
    w/ rat semen

    as he speeds
    toward Cuba
Atomic Enema Devil
Creator of Aids
Square hooligan with
    a Orange S

Where is our why
    our collection
    of questions
    that sizzle like
    beautiful black
    cartoon bombs

    But no one laughs
        at cartoons

They are like us who we are
    carriers
    holders
    receptacles
    vessels
    tools
flat money copping
    scribbles
      Are you cripple?

    Are you the people?

    Does your church have a

                    joke
                  it tells
    a long interesting payment
              of a story

    there myth is welcome
              as green
                  hills
          of Public School
              Mexico

    that it was money, the articulate
          stuffing, and lives
          the history of flashes
                  & gasps. Sudden shut metal
                      doors

                  & bullets whacking
                  into the walls

ODE TO THE CREATURE

I didn't think this was
      the same jungle
      Bushman Bushman
      Nazi dream of Yale
      Bushman Bushman
      hung mouth of blood
      smeared to make eyes
      & mouth
        in the hood

      Bushman
      Bushman
You eat our skin &
          bones
        oh Bushman
        you

     I never wanted to be in Hell
      Yet here we is
        Bushman
        Bushman

    are you the devil
      or just *a* devil?

I didn't care for this beating
        this crazed conversation
        of animal feces

Bushman Bushman
I have asked your picture
to be put on iodine labels

No one, Bushman
wd sleep w/ yr
     cheap greeting card
why haul the dead
        around

why not read the coroner's report

Yr dog is dead

   scribble scribble

X

Everything we dont understand
     is explained
     in Art
     The Sun
    beats inside us
  The Spirit courses in and out
     of us

A circling transbluesency
  pumping Detroit Red inside, deep thru us
      like a Sea
          & who calls us bitter
         has bitten us
         & from that wound
             pours Malcolm
                    Little
                     by
                    Little

I Am

for Addison Gayle, "The Black Aesthetic"
& Abdullah Buhaina

Blues March

We are being told of the greatness
of Western Civilization
Yet Europe
is not the West

Leave England headed West
    you arrive
        in Newark,

The West is
The New World
            not Europe

The West is
        El Mundo Nuevo
        The Pan American
        Complexity
        As diverse as the routes
        & history
        of our collection

The West is The Americas
    not Europe

It is the America that the home
    boy tells, the sister we can
    see, yr wife, husband & children
Yr mama
Yr friends
Yr family
Yr closest enemies

        Are West, The quest
            The Search
            for Humanity
            still goes on

But of the Euro White Supremacists
    The Slave Masters
            Conquistadores
    Destroyers of Pharonic Egypt
                Carthage

Invaders, Destroyers of Moorish Spain
            Of African and Asian Worlds
            Creators of the Inquisition
            Christ Killers
            Murderers of thousands of Christians
                    in the Coliseum
            Murderers of Spartacus
                    Vandals
                    Germ Mens
                    DitchMen
                    Boers

Destroyers of Mohodarenjo
        Tenotchitlan
        Killed Montezuma & Emiliano Zapata
        Malcolm X, Martin Luther King, even
        the Kennedies, Bobby Hutton, Fred Hampton
        Medgar Evers,

            The Aztecs
            The Incas
            The Mayans
            The Taino
            The Arawak

      Conquerors
        of
       America

      Enslaving

       Humanity
        in
       Cannibal
       Menus

      Bush men living on human
        flesh as public
         ritual
         ideology of predators
        & blood covered claws

Murderers of Iraq, wd be destroyers of
the ancient Mesopotamian culture
        Assassins of Sandino
        Toussaint Louverture, Patrice Lamumba

Enslavers of Women
Overthrew Mother Right
Killed Socrates, Copernicus, Lincoln
John Brown & Nat Turner
Amilcar Cabral & David Sibeko

Who claim Civilization & Christianity & Philosophy as
Crucifiers who worshipped statues
till 300 AD

Who destroyed the libraries of Alexandria
the University at Timbuctoo
Who thought the wind made babies

Who say now they are the creators of Great Civilizations
plagiarists, ignorant imitators
claiming Geometry & the Lever

which existed 1000 years before
they was even here
whose great minds are thieves like
Aristotle, Con men like
Democritus & Anaximander
whose Gods are the Vanilla Ice
of Ethiopian Originals
half dressed cave dwellers
painted blue

Anglos (knife wielding) Saxons
Sackers (Robbers) of Ancient Civilizations
Vikings whose Gods were drunk and rowdy
robbers like Conan & Wodan

315

Punks like Napoleon who
got run out of Haiti
    by Toussaint & Dessaline

    who got bum rushed out
        of Russia
    wacked out
    racist monsters
shot the nose & mouth
    off the Sphinx
    so sick &

    anti-life & history were they
        who put Mali & Songhay &
        all Africa
        in Slave Ships

        for money, whose profits
    were numbers not visionaries
    Life as a low thing
worshippers of Mines not Minds
    War Lovers not Peace Makers

    Aint instead of Art
    (Death instead of Life)
        Dog they best friend
            Ice & Snow
    Not We & Know
    Blood Suckers &
                    Mother Fuckers

Love War
so much

call the history
of their civilization

The Canon!

    in honor of Marco Polo's
       trip to China

Should we praise them
    for Dachau, for the poisoning
       of David Walker
        the Genocide of Native
         Americans
        or concentration camps
        for Japanese
         Americans

Perhaps 700 years of Irish Colonialism
       or Gandhi's
        murder
       The Conquest of India
       The Opium Wars
       TB Sheets for
       Indians
    or the trail of Tears

So how should we praise them?
And what should we call them?
       Who style themselves God
       Whose New World Order
       Seems old & Miltonian in that they rule
       & do not serve

But somehow the term Satan seems too narrow
   The word Devil is too limiting

But there must be some description, some appropriate
horrific
      we can coin –

      Something that says liar, murderer, maniac, animal
      something that indicates their importance.

Syncretism

BAD NEWS SAY
KILL
      DRUM
But Drum
no

   die

just
     act   slick

drum turn
 mouth
 tongue

      drum go voice
      be hand
      on over
        hauls
      dont die

      how some ever

drum turn slick

never
no drum
never
never
die

be a piano
    a fiddle
    a nigger tap
      fellah

    drum'll
      yodle
if it need to

Thing say Kill drum
    but drum
          dont die/ dont even
                    disappear

& drum cant die
    & wdn't

        no way!

Tom Ass Clarence

for Ol Black Joe

Ask these knees if there's
a negro attached
to them
Ask these knees
who they belong to
& how long they been here
pinned to the
        ground.

"These knees can talk, child!"
1st time I seen knees talk.
But these knees can talk
These knees can cry
These knees can even lie

Only knees had a program on tv
Only knees married to
       a pornography of naked nuns
Only knees can exist w/o anybody
       w/o no legs or thighs
            or feet or anything
Only knees can exist
       independent
       of anything

completely
by themselves
autonomous

these are
Self made knees

prosperous knees
proud knees
shiny knees

These knees are
      Called
    Knee grows

    Like I sd
    These knees
    be on television
    They got they own
      Show.

CITATION

Now instead of Amos &
  Andy "integration"
  has given us
  The Skip & Spike
    Show
   Straight out of
   Pandora's Box

   Buttermilk covered
    Flies

   Come
   from the busted nut
   of square darkness

   Famous germs
   explaining diseased
   jism
   from the inside

Reichstag 2

How per fect that it was a Muslim
        Fundamentalist, one who shot Meir
        Kahane (and was acquitted) the one
        who was to be deported, one eyed
        priest of an evil violent Muslim
        cult. And it smells like Saddam or
        The PLO, Quadaffi, Khomeini, the death threat
        on Rushdie. Their hatred of Jews, their bloody
        terrorism. And cheap greasy brown foreign
        primitive violence.

The Mossad could do it, with the Serbs, cover the slaughter
        of Muslims in Bosnia. The Spook, Lee,
        explained to niggers, for us, how Nigger
        Muslims killed Malcolm. Farrakhan's
        a Muslim. Elijah Muhammad. Malcolm
        X was a Muslim.

It will be simple, like Americans,
        & greed will become
            moral outrage.

Art Against Art Not

Art Not is Devil Death
Delusion
like emptiness
Silence
the dark
ignorance
That everything that exists

is alive

Whatever there *wasiswill*
Space encompasses, yet the
truth stares from it
invisible as most
of where we are

We are in the body of space
as space
in specific lives
& waves

Like foot prints breathing
you'd have to
Know

as you tune in with everything
possibility exists
alive

But space is filling
nurtures
the child

the sun

Where the history
thrusts as longing
withheld
gravity

bursts

the outcome

the meaning

inside the black hole

memory

grew
the 1st dick

to speak

Space
is speech

the snake of Lightning
Thunder clouds

Black snake the tongue of the world a blue
chord coming the milky way, the jizm
the stars shot out in. The electrical "Yes"
of livingness eternal as truth, beyond ourselves
yet in which we will always be part of however!
In that sudden sea of fire, memory becomes
consciousness, the fetus' tail becomes a solo
low & crawling across the earth, yet wise enough
to introduce the naked "people" to reality
& science. Even against the will of their
cruel invisible (land) Lord who told them that
        ignorance is obedience. Mystery is
Holiness. Expelled from paradise for listening
to the black talking snake, Dick Tongue, Blood is a see
song, the pen and the sword, Question & Answer.
The snake counciled the Whys & The Wise. Moving
like life itself, matter contradicted by motion
yet defining its existence & atom of universal
unity.

    The snake told the truth the invisible priest
hid knowledge to stay powerful. It was he who
brought the apple trees. Wasn't no Apple trees
in Africa before G got invisible & decreed the people be naked

too ignorant to live forever. And re enter inner
space closer to becoming again the consciousness of what
exists, Forever.

Spirit is created & continues through matter. The snake
carries the sun rising up & down, like
the heart beat, like lovers, waves of light
& see. The Snake whose name
begins with the same letter as the Sun, the twisting
rising breath of the world.

Blues
our favorite color
ultra violet
the soul is invisible
when it arrives
turning indigo
as it

  Grows visible
From the light
      of consciousness
       rising
      The Soul
is the Sun's
      History

it comes to understand
    life
    it's loss
    The Blown

The Blowing

The Blue

    Mother Sky

of the transparent

Endlessness

we blow

The Blues

of sky & water

Wherein we wail

to bring forth the sea

the revelation of blow top

Outness

to go into the

Farther

the way out
Trane blows all night

Getting Happy

The Good News just above

The future is the lowest

heaven

comes

So it is the seeds wrapped in a bag

resembling infinity

the tallness

of the next

moment

When we were free

We were blue

but we blew

& became the blues

the beautiful sky & water

the sad song of the Sun

travelin

light

Because the Sun

is Blue

& the world motor

weres

the engine

is history

Whirring

in side

Yet Life became Money

the Green Giant

a television Star

Gold at the Height

orange

at the Fall

O.J.

*

Understand the quest & the mystery.
That the circle, the whole is an entrance
a hole, a slit where from the old tongue
split by contradictions within, the dimension

& isness, what mothers, the me of am continuing
as so connected to everything by getting down
the blues lights the sky orgasm defines
little fish predicting Jesus coming
from inside the womb, the ego
of the earth traveling as mountains & breasts
pointing at the mother from the "gift", the
answer, yr question is a woman creating
the next is, the tale slipping out of the
exclamation of illusion from the mouth
of truth, everything from nothing, the new
like there is silence,
the last refinement
to speak as the sleep of electricity. The
whole, the all ways turns like a full moon
yet who can stare at the sun, the name
of what knew is the reality of "forever".

      The snake was music the visible thought
the answer, as the Sea crawls in waves
the waves of is' story the shared center
What tells nature's needs the real u
the returning self following the soul
back to the right on, the mother
electric exploding measure as
a mirror, the wetness drenches
us with forever as a reflection
of the self's search for consciousness
we can become the matter of understanding
digging itself reexplain the history
of it's actuality, it's life, the
sign in the sky the unseen catching
a glimpse of it's Knowing, which being

is the self of it's will, the route
from which come comes, the forth
dimension which is motion, the on
switch, the self of everything as light
to see the egg on fire with vision
The body of Who, The Yes O Cean
which we leave when smart enough
to confuse naked people
that knowledge is sin

Be is the self twisting & rising & changing
the Beast is King, the body of is "visible" is
so the sea of gestation the waves of light
The I of the snake, history sings the self vision
to be a beast, the soul, anima, as the connector
of truth. What matter/is. Our mother – "life w/o
end", our father, the distance we are from
the creation of the world ourselves as perfect
& alive forever

    To be perfect is to be "invisible" forever
like the inside & outside of the circle. The
Snake lied & became the lion. The naked people
were put out of paradise for believing a snake.
The loins became cloth & sex
mysterious & dirty.

    The tree of Knowledge told them
nothing valuable. Like the Greek tortured
for stealing fire. Socrates poisoned. The Sphinx
sits fixed by her animal lower self. Her
visible self at the top is a woman
There is the soul of what creates, Alma

Mater, staring into the white invisible sky
human connected to no motion by an animal
the King of the Animals, crouching on his tale
headless as King, a powerful beast, who
cannot move disconnect from his eyes

Yesterday a comet fell into Jupiter from
the sky (at thousands of miles a second)
in massive fire balls of explosion
Sun Ra arrives

ANCIENT MUSIC

The main thing
to be against
is *Death*!

Everything Else
is a
Chump!

Getting Down!

Sisyphus explained
why he cant stand
Rock & Roll,

"The Judge sentence me to
the same thing
Then call these freaks
The Rollin Stones
To rub it in."

THE HEIR OF THE DOG

How amazed the crazed
      negro looked informed
      that Animal Rights had
      a bigger budget
      than the NAACP!

INCRIMINATING NEGROGRAPHS

Perceiving Miss

What do you think
of the movie
"X"?

Spike
Lie!

The Ho of Bup

"It was never about
yall. Hey, it was
always about
me

"Single negro on the
country club green
Only negro on the board
of International
Obscene

"Last name, Jackson
1st Name, Gunga Din

Hard shiny slave slobber
is whats left of
my brain

"A Spike Lee Joint" Is A Negro Reefer

It makes believe
It gets you high.

"The Wages of Sin" Explained

Invoke the Nation
   to secure your fortune

Betray the Nation
   to receive your fortune

The X Is Black

(Spike Lie)

If the flag catch
    fire, & an x
    burn in, that x is Black
    & leaves an
    empty space. It
    is that place
    where we live
    the Afro American
    Nation

If the flag
    catch fire
    & a x burn in
    the only stripes is
    on our back
    the only star
    blown free
    in the northern sky
    no red but our
    blood, no white
    but slavers and Klux in hoods
    no blue
    but our songs

If the flag catch fire
        & an x
        burn in
        that x is black
        & the space that is left
        is our history
        now a mystery

we only live
where the flag
is not
where the air is funky
the music
hot
Inside the hole
in the American soul
that space, that place
empty of democracy
we live
inside the burned boundaries
of a wasted symbol
x humans, x slaves, unknown, incorrect
crossed out, multiplying the wealth of others

If the flag
        catch fire
        & an x burn in
        that x
        believe me,
        is black

Fresh Zombies

O<small>K</small> Shuffle. Stink in neon
Lie in lights. Betray before millions
Assassinate w/ slogans. Not old toms
but New Toms, Double Toms
A Tom Tom Macoute. Fresh Zombies
House Nigger maniacs. Oreo serial killers
That thumping, that horrible sound,
is not music, not drums, but shuffling
Not old toms, New Toms, Double toms
A Tom Tom Macoute. Fresh Zombies

Who Killed Malcolm X

The Same people who killed
    Kennedy
    & King
    & Bobby
    & Fred Hampton
    The same ones who
    shot Lumumba
    & Cabral. the same murderer
    cracker imperialism
who killed Bobby Hutton
    or Medgar Evers
    still directly connected
    to the secret government
    that killed Lincoln
    that seceded
    that had slaves
who locked Garvey up & deported him

who attacked & dishonored & lied about
     DuBois
          Who drove him
               to exile

Nat Turner & David Walker were killed
               by the same
               forces

The murderers of Vesey & Gabriel
Who destroyed Robeson
& humiliated Langston & Zora

Who killed
the little girls & blew up
that church
     in Birmingham

Who freed Emmett Till's
          murderers?
Who blew up Ralph Featherstone's
          car?

BAD PEOPLE

We want to be happy
    neglecting
  to check
  the definition

We want to love
    & be loved
      but
      What does that
        mean?

Then you, backed up against
    yr real life

      claim you want
      only
      to be correct.

Imagine the jeers,
    the cat calls
    the universal dis

      such ignorance
      justifiably
      creates.

The Under World

Sd the Mayor
to the councilman,
"I never did respect
a preacher w/out a
church!"

Sd the councilman
to the Mayor,
"I never did respect
a queen w/out a
throne!"

IN THE FUNK WORLD

If Elvis Presley/ is
    King
Who is James Brown,
    God?

Americana

They hate the idea
of love, and disconnect
it from power and intellect
by claiming only 5 senses
& sex.

LOWCOUP*

Craziness is no
        Act
            Not to
                Act

        is crazinezz

*Lowcoup is an Afro American verse form, as Haiku is Japanese!

"ALWAYS KNOW"

— MONK

If the animals
will not leave
of their own/ free
will

And Jesse Jump up
in a Donkey's tale
screaming "Let us Prey!"
Check it out

      He might not / even
        be talkin
          to you!

History Is a Bitch

Can you understand inside the cover you tell
    inside the problems the water falls on you
    it's not rain, there's no God so it's not "their"
    tears, nothing but thin air, in which the nigger
    bops like breath to be a ghost or a churl

I knew you when you didn't exist, a dead island where a few
    weirdos ran sheep. I laughed, the others too, explaining
    the icy fire that held it visible. Post card on
    the shore of a naked man and woman, the snake
    resembled yr mama.

We were a million years old by then & sleek with
    paraphernalia. Laid back under the trees for lunch
    casually noting the germs & their pitiful parrots

They smiled as we approached, like in a zoo with no attendants
    Don't think that twisting Blankness of dead caves
    didn't touch us. But drunk is laughing at it's best
    & the priests winked

Now it's thousands past, the moon & the sun don't even bother
    to appear. It's night they told us, *then,* & we didn't
    understand. oh boy, oh boy. Forget Christ & them

He never even got to Europe. It was a joke then, the
    Tarot spoke of the hanged man, & the
    imitation dancer wd immortalize
    the fool.

Size Places

The unresolved future
The one dimensional delusion
like chauvinism is sickness
      HELL
            He Ill

            He Will

                  Only He.

      2

            it is an exactitude
      how we live, forever, in Hells
            or Heavens

      3

      The constancy
            of infinite motion
            into way
                  Is we are our
      only creators created

by our selves as we are
created by those in It that
created before

4

        Beauty is
More Beautiful
      we dig
than the
Ant Knows.

& Who
by that
Sees us as
tiny ignorant
      animals?

To the Faust Negro to Sell His Soul to the Devil for That Much!

Oh Americans Who Have OverCome
Their Black Skin
But Are Still Sometimes
Confused w/ Afro Americans

Oh, Smart Negroes
Oh, Professional Over Standers
Oh, Sparkling Comfortable
Chattel, Slavemaster Condums
Poison Pus still oozing
from the living sores
of Plantation Leprosy

Oh. Bigtime LARGE LIVING
Corporate, Backward Buppie, Well Trained
Senior Playtoy Puppies, Negroes who have Made It/ Have Made
America Work For Them. Anti Afro American Charismatic Coons
Yo! Generals, Presidents, Deans, Chairs,
Yo! Medical Association Negroes, Tainted Mouthpieces,
Compradors, Quislings
Ubiquitous Rats, Fishy Public Officials, Shadow Sin Aiders
MayWhores, Media Pimps . . .
Dem Negro Crats, Reel Public Coons, Video Demons
        with Grant to act like Lee

Ignorant History Distorting Ho's
expensive important diamond studded
Unisex Skeezers

Oh, glittering monsters blessed by The Supremist Lord
of Imperial
Whiteness

The Invisible god
of
Heathen
Brain Fever
Infection

Poison Fleas
mashed throughout
the
falling
Doo Doo

plummeting
through the Colon
Clarencing
out the Ass

The Heathen "Word"
for feces
is
Tom.

Drop out white behinds
with a low single splat

a fragment B
Flat
The Latest Hit
of Heathen Shit

Disappearing
covered with nasty papers
proving they had once been inside
The A D L's stomach

They spirit is the
BeezleBub
We Nose

Oh Ghosts of Rotten Past

Nice Negroes
reasonable about
    Slavery
armed with the Knee Pads
    of Their Class

        Kneeling
          to
        prey

        The Masters
        Answered
        prayers
        Negro
        Miracles

Created By The Power & Glory of Lies & Violence
Fraud & Force
By the bloody torture of his visible
Avatar the Heathen Cracker

Oh Niggers who love the very hatred of the whip
who sing like the blood cut out our hearts
Oh tap dancing, butt swinging, successful butchershop
mind stinking toilet paper lip well dressed wholly dishonest
souless paper academic flag pole living deformed mouth
woogies who lie through the caucasian chalk circle of their
constant giggle
who speak a language constructed from the masters farts

More and more I have come to believe
you will have to be eliminated
in order for the rest of us
to live.

BLACK RECONSTRUCTION

OH FREEDOM *segue to* BATTLE HYMN OF THE REPUBLIC

What the Doctor explained
    was that we had fought
    that we had patiently
    rushed into our trans
                  formed
selves.

    That we had run away
from the plantations & closed
them down. That we had
plagued our liberators
to let us be liberated.
And offered our whole selves
as proof that God is real.
And we are his children.
And that there is a
Spirit in our suffering
that beats like twilight
red rain brown lit up
with thunder.
I cd see that then,
What that roar within us
the cymbals sharp &

glowing hot, as we put
on blue again, & became
ourselves, where we were,
as the angels in the chariot
ourselves, getting down to
make heaven our home.

That is the way it was told
When we put the Blue on
Again. With yes, the Blue
Steel bayonets, and the speech
of the prophets fashioned
out weapons of fire.

Then that rush, of a Gideon
Screaming madness high up
John Coltrane Savage Nigger
African Explosion Color

That the Freedom! The that
the yeh say what Bam!
Splat volcano language
of Free – Do you, The Free
The Bird – My sign, on my face
the skin raised, to show
out of fire, sky nut sperm
the jism that made the world
all the non stop lovely goodness
unstoppable screaming

It was like the ascension
itself, after 40 days
we were exploded into
the endless inspiration

To understand our lives
as they exist
                in the
                Spirit
                World

    the freedom of
    the always
    happy
    excitement
          of
          Love
          The Good
    The Living Laughter
        of all
            hearts

    to be that as a world
    as the creator
                of worlds

    We knew we wd be saved
    that it was in ourselves
    our understanding
    & acceptance
    of our salvation.

    But the redeemer
    said he was covered
    with blood. Of wolves
    who tried to consume
    the lamb

the black sheep
our souls, Ba Ba
our souls
are in our wool

& mine eyes
bear witness
to the Lord
& the glory of
his coming!

In *The Fugitive*

Richard Kemble kept insisting
he did not kill
his wife. That the real
murderer, was a one-armed
man.   He was telling the truth
all the time. And we knew it!
In the new series, if you watch
television, the real murderer
has become the Republican Senate Majority
Leader, who goes everywhere
with a pet lizard
who defecates through his mouth
& blows hot green gas out his tale.
Which, in certain conditions
oddly resembles low German.

Othello Jr.

(One Moor Time)

$

=

"

A Ne(gr)o Classical
Tragedy

of

"Amusement
& Contempt"

*

The Prologue

in

Three Lowcoup

I

AB, LHing on JEJ, Dig?

If James Earl Jones
    can play
    a Black Man

    Then don't complain
    about Lawrence
    Olivier

    as
    O
Thell
    O,

                OJ?

II

Chris Darden

Othello & You
Othello Jr too
All worked for
The Christians

& like them Jigs
you got the old
gig. In the arena
as entertainment for
Barbarians

Surrounded
by all of em's
Lyins

& yr boy
O Jr
playing
Norman Bates

Making
  Faces
    &
      Screaming in Stares,

"You got my soul!
  I sold you my soul!

"I'll Kill to keep my Balls!

  III

If OJ is Othello
       Jr

& Vermin
is Iago

Marsha Clarke
Desdemona

& Cato
doofus Cassio

Johnny C.
The Man
who ran out
on his father

Chris
     the
         Arena's Prey

     Preying
     for Civilization

       Then
     Othello was Called
to go out & greet
     Hell
     & Fight
     for it.

     In love with
     Gold
     Enthralled by
     Otherness!

     But there is a
       Venice
       in California
Where the Punic Wars
       Rage on

& there
       Moorish
           Women
               freed
                 his
                     Son!

FUNK'S MEMORY

Plays on & on place after place into futures past
It's passing It the is the is was been & going
Going is blowing gone is blown
Why the Funk remember
Why the Funk keep all we hearts

Like marching could be wind & noises
Like falling could be song
Like rising could be fire & lit skies
Like loving could be Music
never denied

All them to come was here when they left
    all us who left here is now
        about to come
            cause we in love
                what keep us breathing
                    is keep us a spirit
                        a point to pointing
                            a go to going
                                & we keep coming
                                    Oh baby, is nightime
                                        Joe Williams say nightime
                                        is the right time

And it's like wind and cool blue &
    a life of pictures
        everything always
            alive.

FUNK LORE

Blue Monk

We are the blues
    ourselves
    our favorite
     color
    Where we been, half here
                 half gone

We are the blues
    our selves
    the actual
     Guineas
    the original
     Jews
    the 1st
     Caucasians

That's why we are the blues
    ourselves
    that's why we
     are the
     actual
      song

So dark & tragic
    So old &
        Magic

    that's why we are
        the Blues
        our Selves

  In tribes of 12
    bars
  like the stripes
    of slavery
      on
    our flag
    of skin

We are the blues
    the past the gone
    the energy the
    cold the saw teeth
    hotness
    the smell above
    draining the wind
    through trees
    the blue
    leaves us
    black
    the earth
    the sun
    the slowly disappearing
    the fire pushing to become
    our hearts

& now black again we are the
whole of night
with sparkling eyes staring
down
like jets
    to push
    evenings
    ascension
    that's why we are the blues
    the train whistle
    the rumble across
    the invisible coming
    drumming and screaming
    that's why we are the
    blues
    & work & sing & leave
    tales & is with spirit
    that's why we are
        the blues
        black & alive
        & so we show our motion
            our breathing
            we moon
            reflected soul

    that's why our spirit
      make us

      the blues

    we is ourselves

      the blues

One Thursday I Found This in My Notebook

When love is perfected, when love
    is understood.
  When love is the law
      & the measure
    The ruler & ruled & body of
      of what is body mind of
      what is mind
    When love & the Soul
      are uncovered
   then you will always
     sound like
        Duke Ellington.

DUKE'S WORLD

Passion Flower
for "Strays"

is the explanation
beauty makes
the look of understanding
a new day being so ancient
brings

There is an ascendance in Duke. A passage
through which you are pulled, where everything
that lives forever regards itself & lets you know
you can be there always when you are beautiful

There is no ugliness that describes Duke's world
except what is not
& how it connects to
what is

It is not just the elegance, the irony, the
sensuous self illumination
there is also deep happiness
in Duke's world

What you think is a castle, expansive gardens
is a teacher impeccably in love with
exaltation & joy. Duke's world
is where we go if we are good.

Afro American Talking Drum

Duke

If you got real spooky
& became Duke Ellington
America wd deny it
just like they did
to the real Duke
Ellington

Ellingtonia

Duke
      speaks for everybody
& the Devil
      resents
         this!

It disturbed me
      so much

I was determined
      to ask him, the
            Devil,

Why this was
    So. Why did he resent

       Duke Ellington?

The Devil, not being a
        racist,
      explained

       (& in a very convincing
           way)

        that he didn't mind
          Duke
        it was his
          music
        that he
          despised!

MONK'S WORLD

'Round Midnight

That street where midnight
is round, the moon flat
& blue, where fire engines solo
& cats stand around & look
is Monk's world

When I last saw him, turning around
high from 78 RPM, growling
a landscape of spaced funk

When I last spoke to him, coming out
the Vanguard, he hipped me to
my own secrets, like Nat
he dug the numbers & letters
blowing through the grass
initials & invocations of the past

All the questions I asked Monk He
answered first
in a beret. Why was
a high priest staring
Why were the black keys
signifying. And who was
wrapped in common magic

like a street empty of everything
except weird birds

The last time Monk smiled I read
  the piano's diary. His fingers
  where he collected yr feelings
  The Bar he circled to underscore
  the anonymous laughter of smoke
  & posters.

Monk carried equations he danced at you.
What's happening?" We said, as he dipped &
  spun. "What's happening?"

"Everything. All the time.
  Every googoplex
  of a second."

Like a door, he opened, not disappearing
  but remaining a distant profile
  of intimate revelation.

Oh, man! Monk was digging Trane now
  w/o a chaser he drank himself
  in. & Trane reported from
  the 6th or 7th planet deep in

  the Theloniuscape.

Where fire engines screamed the blues
  & night had a shiny mouth
  & scatted flying things.

BUDDHA ASKED MONK

"If you were always right
    would it be Easier
    or more Difficult
    Living In The World?"

"I knew you'd ask that!"
    Monk said, Blue and
    Invisible.

Monk Zen

Monk
always
come in a
    place
later.
      Long after you first see
      him
      come in.

People say they
      didn't see him
      leave –

Miles say
      So What?

Monk say
      Well, You Needn't

Wilbur Ware say
      Me & Shadow & Trane was wit him when he went out
      You musta heard us!

Lullaby of Avon Ave.

I used to walk past Sassy's crib
a couple times a week, when young

And each time say, "That's
Where Sarah Vaughn lives".

That was when Symphony Sid
used to call her, "The Divine One",
Late nights, from hip Bird Land

Oh man, what a feeling that was
Divine & so hip & so very
beautiful.

The house is gone now
Symphony Sid too

As for the town, now
Sassy told us
just before she split

I'm gone, now
Send in

The
Clowns!

The Dark Is Full of Tears

When Albert returned from
the grave, he had no horn. He
asked us to look for it &
we agreed.

He sd he wd return when
we found it. He was somewhere
in space, drugged about Religion
& The Mob.

I asked him had he been
murdered.

"Of course", Albert wd answer
most things like this though,

"Murdered by God! That's why
it was stupid to believe
in him!"

Fusion Recipe

Take a pinch of
        quote R & B

Add a smidgen/ of
        quote Jazz

Combine in a very shal
        low/ mildly heat
                ed/ Crock
      of "Uncle Sam" brand
                  bovine fecal
                        sauce
Then let the mixture sit
until it turns
        to
           cheap furniture.

JA ZZ : (THE "SAY WHAT?") IS IS JA LIVES

Yes Bees !

God-Electric

Come Coming

Fire Jism

S H A N G O

CANTO JONDO

Eternity Power

Living Happiness

S P I R I T   L I F E

WORD SHIP

The Soul's Soul
SUN   THOUGHT   BREATH

Heart Beat

Is Going

Act Play

Ecstasy's   Now

Connecting   Endlessness

REAL   TRUE

LOVE   ALWAYS

SOUND   ARE

D I G G E R   D I G G I N G

THE

WHO   BE

THE

WHAT   WATT

2

Seer   Seeing

SO   U   NeeDn't

THE KEY
of
M O N K

M U N T U   K U N T U

The Laughing South
NIGHT'S MOTHER
The Crying North
DEY FATHER

"Two Is One"

bottom to Top

Hot to Cold

new to Old

See Navy

Sea Crosser

Trance Former

Passing going

The
I   Am

The Am Eye

R

B'

ZZ

The Silence of Sound

The Power
of Universal
Orgasm

The Sun's
Nut
The Thunder The Lightning

The Two Hands

The Dialectic

WHO
WHERE

The You & I
of Here & There

THE DOWN UP

THE BLUE MAN

WHO

THE WOMB MAN

THE HUE MAN

WHO

Both
Yall
  we
I & I

  The
US   IS

I am   Sings

The Sun God
Coming out
      His
      Mother

The Ejaculator
is The Ejaculation!

Come Music!

Visible Thought Herding

In Walked Dionysius

The Pyramid
change to
The Triangular Trade

      The Spell
The Word

Good News
Hip Gnosis

Ghost Murder

Eat Mo
The Grain Crusher
            The Be er
                  The Alle
The Me
See

The See Me
The Me Sea
Waves

NIGHT BLUE
    DAZE
THE DERE DAT

The Eye
On

 The

  DEATH DEAD!

 The Living Knowing

  THE
  STAY GO

  CHURCH SPEECH

 The STING
Of
  NIGGER PRINTS

  MOON'S SON

   YOU
   I

 The So
  &
 The So

 The Where

  the
 were so

the
Sower

Gravity
The Meaning

the
GO
How

The blue
blown
The Blues
what we blew

Hawk Honk
Black Bird Aflame

The smile rising
the changes the circle
the hole

The Whole

The Hard Empty

The upside down
the twist to
frown

The cold circle checker
The hot opposite the cross the water, before whatnot

the dooji
the vonhz

other stuff
flying anyway

the chord you came in on

The To Where
        The Every
                The body of joy

                The Why

                The Or

        Elgeba's Cymbal

        The Y he show you
        Yes, The Cross Roads

                G's Us
                the stiff joint
                The hot poem
                Volcano balls
                The planets humming

The head circle
the lost ankh
The Resurrection
What John Said
Revelations

We are alive
We are humans
ruled by heathens

Trying to Remember the formula
for killing ghosts

The underground
dark blue speed
star checking

black freedom lady
the kiss of light

the orchestra sky
comet language

africamemorywhisper

blowing
the blown the known
what we knew

what we blew
blues loves us
our spirit is ultraviolet

what we knew
drumwhich

the long measure
my man
treehip
her son

Becoming the One

FASHION THIS
1996–2013

Note to AB

I became a poet
Because every thing
Beautiful seemed
"poetic" to me.
I thought there were things
I didn't understand
that wd make the world
poetry. I felt I knew
who I was but had to
Struggle, to catch up
w/ my self.
Now I do see me
sometimes, a few worlds
ahead, & I speed up, then,
put my head down,
Stretch my stride out
& dig
There me go, I scat &
sing, there me go.

TENDER ARRIVALS

Where ever something breathes
Heart beating the rise and fall
Of mountains, the waves upon the sky
Of seas, the terror is our ignorance, that's
Why it is named after our home, earth
Where art is locked between
Gone and Destination
The destiny of some other where and feeling
The ape knew this, when his old lady pulled him up
Off the ground. Was he grateful, ask him he's still sitting up
    there
Watching the sky's adventures, leaving two holes for his own. Oh
    sing
Gigantic burp past the insects, swifter than the ugly Stanleys on
    the ground
Catching monkey meat for Hyenagators, absolute boss of what
    does not
Arrive in time to say anything. We hear that eating, that doo
    dooing, that
Burping, we had a nigro mayor used to burp like poison zapalote
Waddled into the cave of his lust. We got a Spring Jasper now, if
    you don't like that
woid, what about courtesan, dreamed out his own replacement
    sprawled

Across the velvet cash register of belching and farting, his knick names when they

let him be played with. Some call him Puck, was love, we thought, now a rubber

Flat blackie banged across the ice, to get past our Goli, the Africannibus of memory.

Here. We have so many wedged between death and passivity. Like eyes that collide

With reality and cannot see anything but the inner abstraction of flatus, a

biography, a car, a walk to the guillotine, James The First, Giuliani the Second

When he tries to go national, senators will stab him, Ides of March or Not. Maybe

Both will die, James 1 and Caesar 2, as they did in the past, where we can read about

The justness of their assassinations

As we swig a little brew and laugh at the perseverance

Of disease at higher and higher levels of its elimination.

We could see anything we wanted to. Be anything we knew how to be. Build

anything we needed. Arrive anywhere we should have to go. But time is as stubborn

as space, and they compose us with definition, time place and condition.

The howlees the yowlees the yankees the super left streamlined post racial ideational

chauvinists creeep at the mouth of the venal cava. They are protesting fire and

Looking askance at the giblets we have learned to eat. "It's nobody's heart", they

say, and we agree. It's the rest of some things insides. Along with the flowers, the
grass, the tubers, the river, pieces of the sky, earth, our seasoning, baked
throughout. What do you call that the anarchist of comfort asks,
Food, we say, making it up as we chew. Yesterday we explained language.

NOTE FROM THE REAL WORLD

Trail ers form dark story night
trails of dark cloud see ings
in built
out built, to it self's per fection
a renegade
a green glowing shoe
the antidote to the void

nothing but forms
content of revolution
see change
it turns a drop of acid, inside out
it milks a bird of god symbolism, the golden hawk
oba, father,
hawk, god from the fertile crescent
glowing star
the troops rumbling and their horses rumbling
the first junkie is a flea, passing into superior consciousness
in that e poch
at that parallel, a pyramid
at that pyramid a blood dressed in triangular apron
a rod and staff
the world is a newsflash
we are with god when he creates

the stories the poems of the magic city
the night congregates in its birth. Drama.
Roach. Scepter. House. They come down together.

We are the smiler at all that passes and it draws you in,
dreamer
the 9th incarnation of
Vishnu
Was Bull Moose Jackson

CHAMBER MUSIC

There might be someone you love, some one you
wanted to be with, and then, found your self
with, there were such things, such lives and
lovers. I am like that sometimes, I think, some
distant romantic wrapped in music. I wanted to know
myself, and found that was a lifetime's work, the
twists and zig zags, dips and turns, all could
disorient you, that you were no longer you but
somebody else masquerading as yourself's desire.
Rain could come. The sky grow light. It could even be
twilight, in a foreign town. Where you walked under
far noises of invisible worlds. But when you remember
all of your faces, blown now gone forever in the wind,
you'll see that you were always wanting to be you,
you were always wanting to know and love yourself, and you
found a few faces, a few names, that extended your life
into other lives, and as time marches, hours, days, decades
dance, you'll find your hand in someone else's hand, you'll
hear yourself thinking about some person other than you
and then look up and yes there will be some other person
some closeness and echoed tenderness, that make us more than dots
under the far away, that make us more than split seconds of
light

Ars Gratia Artis

I would see
sometimes, shadows spooks
unoriginal deities, fastened
in the dark to my dark, there
alone somewhere, or even in the midst
of other life, people talking, profound
criss cross and imaginative sighs, we
they wd see, someone, it was me, probably
and the ghosts and monsters of all was here
ever, returned, to dance their historic
monster log. Dinosaurs and ape men, saber toothed
philosophers, pranced ugly in my mind, no, in my
room, fuck a mind, they were there, everywhere!
I'd compose music, for the motherfuckers
lonesome for light, backed against shadows,
I'd hum for these fiery red bastards out of hell
I'd sing, Monastic melodies, yeh, Monkish tunes
to the outside of thought, the far side of anything.
And they'd dance, and keep on dancing, they'd dance
and dance, get down all night. That's how I became
a poet, singer against terror blue black red terror
in the ghostly midnights of the central ward. That
was my first exposure to literature, coming right

out my mouth, them hot serenades
to keep the ghosts away. My poetry, then,
has always been aimed at destroying ugly shit.
So why, Ronald Reagan, shd you get away?

Oklahoma Enters the Third World

After the bombing,
                    I saw Americans
                    on television

their faces exiled from
the candy brain-destroying
fraud, fakery & Madness
of their culture.

They did not look like
Kewpie Dolls or the ads

        their faces were pulling away
from the money-dick slavery
klan wax nazi white
supremacy primitive cave
savage airbrushed, violent
greedy ignorant culture.

The wax faces melted with their
eyes, and they, for a moment, felt
the truth.
And for that moment came

into the world, & like most
of the rest of us
in the world.

They were actually, crying.

Got Any Change?

Instead of this street
With its wasted brothers
Asleep on the corners
So the crack jackers
Have to step over them
W/ the cuss out laugh
Of the soon to be wasted
Themselves.

Instead of this street
In a city, where aint nothin
Pretty, but the people
Who keep on standing
& really laughing &
actually underneath our night
make love to each other
even if they fight.

A city ruled by a Negro
Ghoul, a sepia Lieutenant Nazi
With licence to fool, a looney
Tunes coon, so skilled
At deception, everything he thinks
Is a lie, and he has had his

Snoring altered to resemble
Casual remarks

We are in New Ark, the Brick
          City, Like I sd
Where only the people
          Are pretty
& they have a hell of a
          time being that

Ruled by his dishonor, the May Whore
Who has crowned
Hese'f Emperor, His Majesty
The Rat

Ghost brain
In a rubber brown
"Black Man" costume
Like TB spit.
He sick, always laughing
To cover the fact he has no face.

& Like post Dallas JFK look for his brain
aint even a trace

So we have climbed the ladder
To this, where white folks
Seem to recede to the margins
Of our pain, and their
Black substitutes are prostitutes

And clinically insane.

We are being taught about classes
And class struggle
& the people of whatever color
are not what they look like
but exactly how they act, a cold fact

We are in a city ruled by
A mad nigger punk
A Mobutu, Abacha
Backward petty bourgeois
Heels and Scum

Who serve imperialism &
Corporate rule,
Who hate Black People
Any poor people
They are well made tools

We must overthrow
These negro asst. beasts
Loathsome things
For whom evil is sexual release

Are they puppets? Ask them?
They'll tell you they aint no such thing
They're just very very smart, you know,
They get to help the rulers pull their strings.

Negroes like Sharpe James from the most backward

Between Infra-Red & Ultra-Violet

We are the inside of reality, what move it and turn it up
Around and on on, we are the where you been and the there
You go, we ain't perfect, we ain't even rich, we ain't that
    believable sometime, what we
want. What we say, all the upside inside by George they went
    off like that, stuff.

We are the silent and the loud. The quiet blue in the sky of
    morning, the murmuring
Redness makes when the sun books to light up the rest of the
    family.
We are old as anything but never stay anywhere too long. We
    invented whatever you
Can say, except we dont want to take credit for bad shit, but
    we invented that
Too. My man over there invented God, on a humble, under a
    tree and jimmy dropped
A load on his head. He said God and that got over for dough.
    My wife invented
Bread, from flowers. I said it was a good idea then went off
    trying to bite a tree. I
Climbed up in a tree second. She was first. I invented
    quizzical expressions and long
Silences. I thought up music the way the sky wanted to get in
    our business all the Time.

We are everywhere you been and where you going we let you
     know to go there. Your
boy in the corner sleep invented the devil and got his behind
     whipped by his own
theory. Then tried to lock up what it brought. He invented
     jails too and was the first
one in one. The dude over there crying invented the church
     now he trying to explain
what he meant.

We are the fall as it lets you dig it. The spring as you walk
     through it smiling. We are
Rain. Light and heavy. And fire when it simmers under our
     food. I thought up speech
When my toe got broke trying to eat a flower. The sky I used
     to call sister All and
Thought Shango was doing it do her. I got here second. My
     wife was first. I wanted to keep on hunting on the ground.
     Till the bite marks made me look like one of them ugly
     cats who wanna sink they teeth in your next is.

We were here when anybody thought to think up being here.
     We was invited to be
Humans and thought we had copped. We was communists
     covered with our natural
Vines. Let it go for groceries. Then had to cut out when the
     grocer got ugly.

We was big fish and could sing then. We was wailing in the
     water, and dug light was
In the waves. We explained tides and kept records when Bird
     was jet black and
Crisscrossed overhead chasing the sun. We figured out what
     the soul was watching
Him. I could sing when my fingers come out.

412

We lived everywhere there is, and know everything but what
    we need to know next.
We the only people never been nowhere that don't exist. We
    dream in the billions.
Your boy, the dog with the hat on, invented money. That's
    why he got a gun. He say
Somebody wanna waste him.

We are the shadows that haunt what shouldn't stay around.
    We are the whispers of
The future's wings. The engines of the spirit, the breath of
    the earth, the dirt, the lips
Of the water. The beating of the day night day night. I come
    here second. Where was I
Before? Before is not anybody you know. I used to play the
    drums when they growed
Up in my hand. I sat in a tree and thought up numbers. I was
    a revolutionary from
way back, ask that cat with my bad talk in his ear and new foot
    up his ass. I confess
Evil was an experiment. Don't hold it against me. I knew it
    was risky and told your boy
Jacoub. He dug it later and started a singing group.

We was so out we went away and came back to go again and
    made a circle to have
Something to say. Eating was the way we walked. I was never
    alone I come here
Second, my wife was first.

We know what need to be and keep talking about it. We is
    singers and drummers and

Horn players and poets and painters and sculptors and
    dancers and actors and
Workers and runners. My man over there thought up flying
    but then had to come
back when he went to where he started. We was planets and
    stars. We was notes and
rests. We walked before the clouds asked us to. We was hungry
    before we knew
about food.

We is revolutionary day into night into star into somewhere
    look up we coming again.
We is you too. We is two you. We is come and gone coming
    and going. Loving and
digging, laughing and copping. Listening and singing.
    Dancing and timing. We is
space and time as a picture card of everything we is
    revolutionaries. The world is not
what it will be. We is what will make it that and then. We is the
    never of the yes/ the
tiny of the grand. The hotness of the coolth. The seeing of
    the believing the practice of
the theory. The history of the future. The lost of the found we
    are what you need and
what you get if you stay around. We are what we was when you
    are where you going.
And was still getting down. We was perfect and rejected it for
    travel we is with you
we is you we is us and you we is you and you is everything all
    of us is one family one
thing one mother & father. One everyall one never not/ We is
    the revolutionaries We
is the earth turning we is the stars coming we is the hot rising
    the cold descending.
We is we is we is we is is is is we

In The Theater

Earth is the visible
    representation
      of
    ⎣is⎦ ⎡is⎤

    matter in motion

the concrete
    materiality of
    true
    being
    real
    consciousness
    Ever
     in
     Fact

The Science of Knowing

    The Dance

    The Unity
    of Opposites

the nature
of nature

Dialectical

with the Play of contradictions
turning inside and outside
each other
becoming something
else

The Drama of Yes & No
Two Masques dividing the whirl,
Who rise from the bottom possessed by Ecstasy
Who fall from the top dragged by Tragedy

Africa's Blue Laughter
Europes Gray Tears

OUTSANE

1

The price
  Of being here
  Is Knowing
As if Blindness
  Was music
  You hated

But you can see
  & you hear it
  like yr breath

Each day whines
  Bluely open
  Redly closed

Images unseen
  Unheard
  Except
  Knowing
  Is worse
  Proof

2

Every thing is a
            Knowing
  & a No-ing
            it is what it is
            defined by what
                it is not
& at the same time
            becoming & not
                            coming A being is itself
            a Knowing
            a How
            it is that
matter & fact
            & it's qualities
                connect & dis
                connect
            resemble &
            unresemble

Everything is a cure
            & a sickness
            The Devil say
            "God is Ill
"& Greedy
"& a Lie

"Like
  God cdda stopped
Evil. He cdda

Killed me. Instead
He just claim Good
And I got the leftovers

You wanna get rid of shadows
You got to lock up
The Sun

The Education of the Air

They said they don't want anything or
    Any body. They were lying, and they
    Knew it. They knew they were telling
    The truth. You and I know they were
    Telling the truth. But then how could they
    Be lying. How could they be lying?

    First, the older world, is turned back again
And the people who rule it are neither women
    Nor men. They are inside a thing, inside it. And who
Ask for them sees nothing but tilted shadows, lying, made of
    brick or
Paper. They are inside the other things you cannot see, or if
    you see them
They see you first and have already planned your death or
    imprisonment.

Sometimes they will imprison you in paper or words, or
    sometimes
They will imprison you inside yourself. Where you be
    screaming but
Cannot hear yourself. Such as it be. Such as you cannot see.
    Call me
A black whole, call the world a mystery. So when he said that
    he wanted

Nothing and nobody he was telling the "truth" as far as he
knew it.
But clearly he did not know it.

Did the truth know him? The truth could speak but it was
drowned by itself
As Evil. Evil speaks the truth and so do lies. Sometimes the lie
is truer
Than the truth. Because many times the truth is a lie. And a lie
Is the truth. Get it!

So he lived alone with his own truth lying. And the lie was
clearly true.
Or have you ever, one day, have you never, the next day. Like
standing
On the corner for thirty-five years expecting to be shot. But nothing.
So you go back home and the corner comes in the door
behind you.
And there you are not shot then shot.

So be found out he had been lying by telling the truth as he
knew it.
But not knowing he didn't know he knew a lie as the truth.
So when he found out, he found in. When he opened his eyes
His mouth opened too. He was calling, and this was startling.
He was calling. It was shocking. Because he had never known
He was calling. But he had been calling all the time. And never
Knew it.

He was calling when he discovered he was calling, for what he
Said he didn't want. Thing and Body. Every not any. All things
And all bodies. It was true he had always been calling, Even though
He didn't know it, even though he didn't hear himself. Even though
He was lying when he was convinced he was telling the truth

421

Every Full Moon

I get horrible letters
From Ghosts

Demanding
Money
I pay them
Because there are no laws
Against *Instortion*
The legal term for "Threatening
Demands for Money, &c
Made by Dead People."

But if you burn
These "Williams"
's what the Ghosts
call 'em,)

& say the same words
Mantan Moreland
Used to,
when he was
pulling Security
For Charlie Chan's
"Number One Son"

"Oh Oh!

Oh Oh!

Oh Oh!"

THREE TIMES!

The Ghosts might not stop sending them letters
Right Away

But they probably wont be able
to Find Out
Where you went to!

SOMEBODY BLEW UP AMERICA

They say it's some terrorist,
some barbaric
A Rab,
in Afghanistan
It wasn't our American terrorists
It wasn't the Klan or the Skin heads
Or the them that blows up nigger
Churches, or reincarnates us on Death Row
It wasn't Trent Lott
Or David Duke or Giuliani
Or Schundler, Helms retiring

It wasn't
The gonorrhea in costume
The white sheet diseases
That have murdered black people
Terrorized reason and sanity
Most of humanity, as they pleases

They say (who say?)
Who do the saying
Who is them paying
Who tell the lies
Who in disguise

Who had the slaves
Who got the bux out the Bucks

Who got fat from plantations
Who genocided Indians
Tried to waste the Black nation

Who live on Wall Street
The first plantation
Who cut your nuts off
Who rape your ma
Who lynched your pa

Who got the tar, who got the feathers
Who had the match, who set the fires
Who killed and hired
Who say they God & still be the Devil

Who the biggest only
Who the most goodest
Who do Jesus resemble

Who created everything
Who the smartest
Who the greatest
Who the richest
Who say you ugly and they the goodlookingest

Who define art
Who define science

Who made the bombs
Who made the guns

Who bought the slaves, who sold them

Who called you them names
Who say Dahmer wasn't insane

Who? Who? Who?

Who stole Puerto Rico
Who stole the Indies, the Philippines, Manhattan
Australia & The Hebrides
Who forced opium on the Chinese

Who own them buildings
Who got the money
Who think you funny
Who locked you up
Who own the papers

Who owned the slave ship

Who run the army

Who the fake president
Who the ruler
Who the banker

Who? Who? Who?

Who own the mine
Who twist your mind
Who got bread
Who need peace
Who you think need war

Who own the oil
Who do no toil
Who own the soil
Who is not a nigger
Who is so great ain't nobody bigger

Who own this city

Who own the air
Who own the water

Who own your crib
Who rob and steal and cheat and murder
and make lies the truth
Who call you uncouth

Who live in the biggest house
Who do the biggest crime
Who go on vacation anytime

Who killed the most niggers
Who killed the most Jews
Who killed the most Italians
Who killed the most Irish
Who killed the most Africans
Who killed the most Japanese
Who killed the most Latinos

Who? Who? Who?

Who own the ocean
Who own the airplanes
Who own the malls

Who own television
Who own radio

Who own what ain't even known to be owned
Who own the owners that ain't the real owners

Who own the suburbs
Who suck the cities
Who make the laws

Who made Bush president
Who believe the confederate flag need to be flying
Who talk about democracy and be lying

Who the Beast in Revelations
Who 666
Who know who decide
Jesus get crucified

Who the Devil on the real side
Who got rich from Armenian genocide

Who the biggest terrorist
Who change the bible
Who killed the most people
Who do the most evil
Who don't worry about survival

Who have the colonies
Who stole the most land
Who rule the world

Who say they good but only do evil
Who the biggest executioner

Who? Who? Who?

Who own the oil
Who want more oil
Who told you what you think that later you find out a lie

Who? Who? Who?

Who found Bin Laden, maybe they Satan
Who pay the CIA,
Who knew the bomb was gonna blow
Who know why the terrorists
Learned to fly in Florida, San Diego

Who know why Five Israelis was filming the explosion
And cracking they sides at the notion

Who need fossil fuel when the sun ain't goin' nowhere

Who make the credit cards
Who get the biggest tax cut
Who walked out of the Conference
Against Racism
Who killed Malcolm, Kennedy & his Brother
Who killed Dr King, Who would want such a thing?
Are they linked to the murder of Lincoln?

Who invaded Grenada
Who made money from apartheid

Who keep the Irish a colony
Who overthrow Chile and Nicaragua later

Who killed David Sibeko, Chris Hani,
the same ones who killed Biko, Cabral,
Neruda, Allende, Che Guevara, Sandino,

Who killed Kabila, the ones who wasted Lumumba,
    Mondlane,
Betty Shabazz, Die, Princess Di, Ralph Featherstone,
Little Bobby

Who locked up Mandela, Dhoruba, Geronimo,
Assata, Mumia, Garvey, Dashiell Hammett, Alphaeus Hutton

Who killed Huey Newton, Fred Hampton,
Medgar Evers, Mikey Smith, Walter Rodney,
Was it the ones who tried to poison Fidel
Who tried to keep the Vietnamese Oppressed

Who put a price on Lenin's head

Who put the Jews in ovens,
and who helped them do it
Who said "America First"
and ok'd the yellow stars

Who killed Rosa Luxemburg, Liebknecht
Who murdered the Rosenbergs
And all the good people iced,
tortured, assassinated, vanished

Who got rich from Algeria, Libya, Haiti,
Iran, Iraq, Saudi, Kuwait, Lebanon,
Syria, Egypt, Jordan, Palestine,

Who cut off peoples hands in the Congo
Who invented Aids
Who put the germs
In the Indians' blankets
Who thought up "The Trail of Tears"

Who blew up the Maine
& started the Spanish American War
Who got Sharon back in Power
Who backed Batista, Hitler, Bilbo,
Chiang Kai Chek

Who decided Affirmative Action had to go
Reconstruction, The New Deal,
The New Frontier, The Great Society,

Who do Tom Ass Clarence Work for
Who doo doo come out the Colon's mouth
Who know what kind of Skeeza is a Condoleeza
Who pay Connelly to be a wooden negro
Who give Genius Awards to Homo Locus
Subsidere

Who overthrew Nkrumah, Bishop,
Who poison Robeson,
who try to put Du Bois in Jail
Who frame Rap Jamil Al Amin, Who frame the Rosenbergs,
Garvey,

The Scottsboro Boys,
The Hollywood Ten

Who set the Reichstag Fire

Who knew the World Trade Center was gonna get bombed
Who told 4000 Israeli workers at the Twin Towers
To stay home that day
Why did Sharon stay away?

Who? Who? Who?

Explosion of Owl the newspaper say
The devil face cd be seen

Who make money from war
Who make dough from fear and lies
Who want the world like it is
Who want the world to be ruled by imperialism and national
oppression and terror violence, and hunger and poverty.

Who is the ruler of Hell?
Who is the most powerful

Who you know ever
Seen God?

But everybody seen
The Devil

Like an Owl exploding
In your life in your brain in your self
Like an Owl who know the devil

All night, all day if you listen, Like an Owl
Exploding in fire. We hear the questions rise
In terrible flame like the whistle of a crazy dog

Like the acid vomit of the fire of Hell
Who and Who and WHO who who
Whoooo and Whooooooooooooooooooooooo!

MISTERIOSO 666

Devil walked up
              On Thelonius,
Monk

     Inventing
       The Break Dance

                                   "Hey!"
The Devil say
                                   "Hey!"
Monk left elbow

                         reply

"What's that shit?"
     Devil
          signify

               "Humph"
This dude gonna make me lose
       My high'
               Monk Stopped his shit
       & walked

          away.

434

"Another Lame"
            Was all
                        He say.

IN HELL'S KITCHEN

"Monk,
        if you
        run into
Jesus
Ask him

        Cd he set fire
to a Bush
One Mo Time?"

"Man,
Jesus been dead!

        And God
ain't
        Count Basie!"

12:00 TSMT

I could think

                Around
                  Midnight

We got put
        In the boat

        I don't really
         know remember

        I might do
        Got sense to

I could think
        Around Midnight
        We got here

                    From
                  The Way Off
                        We was

Left was left is left be left
        Till wrong right

Was Red before I read
Black before that
Mind memory
Turn me Blue

I could feel that, Monk did

He could think Midnight
Was deep & dark
Even Blacker
            Than we
            & things around us
            was quiet

Things Alive you couldn't see

        So Monk composed
        Epistrophe!

Well You Needn't

"Are you
      Thelonius Monk?"
         The Conductor
           Asked?

"I already
      answered
         that!"
           Monk said.

Looking at his
      Wrist
         Like he had
           A watch.

Tragic Funny Papers

Remember that
    Little devil
        Gerald 2X
      Created
    (Like Jacoub)

In the pages of
Muhammad Speaks?

    Remember them pointy ears
& the two Dracula fangs
hung out each side
      of his cartoonish mouth?

He was in the Black Muslim newspaper
    Every week like
        He was in jail.

    Then he vanished . . .
Why? No one cd tell!

    Well, he done
      Comeback

& this is some bad news,
Black!

Now he in the white house
A devilish resident
A counterfeit president

Pretending to be human

So that cute little tail
He had

Dangling from his bowel

Is now disguised as the tongue
In the mouth of Colon Powell

Who Is You?

Verse Drama

Who is who?

Who is You?

I is I and me and the you you asked who is you

There. I thought so. A runt

What is a runt?

A runt is something moving fast then stopping abruptly. The T is the ceiling, a sky dimensioning what runt is.

No, no, you missed understand by several shades. I is still running, upward and onward, in fact I cd be called a running.

Oh, you are into language. The "ing", representing You I Self connecting N, with new birth; the mysterious god of money and power

Discourse. I is the on of on going and gone. Up and away

Are you Clark Kent?

Lemme See. Clark, the scribe, well in a way. Kent,
Connected . . . well yes . . . ha ha, well connected

Is the connected emphasizing the Con or the Nec? Is the
ending the sky of gone or is it an email ending for some
institution, dropping the you.

All, both, any way you say that makes me toppermost in the
uttermost

You're, then, not a ghost?

How cd I be a ghost and you see me?

Why do you think I see you?

Are you talking to air?

That's what you think, that I'm talking to You?

Oh, boy . . . be serious

I'm not that high yet. Serious is as far out as we can see and
still be here in Africa You can see me though, cant you

Of course not. I smell you. I feel you. I almost understand
you. But See you, that's pretty far out. No I know you
are there, I see your clothes, your words clogging the
thoroughfares of thought. But see you . . . well perhaps, but
only through a glass

You're quoting the bible. I thought you were an atheist?

I don't shrink from titles others lay out. Atheist if that suits
your trumpet and tin can.

Do you believe in God or not?

I know you're not God. And I don't believe in anything that's
immaterial. Ideas are reflections of material life. Why are you
representing yourself as the big G?

Ha ha, I got G's but I aint he . . . ha ha . . . Well, do you
believe in Spirit?

Of course, that's how I picked yr whatnot up out the ether. Yr
grinding big boy ugly twizzle . . . like a raw acid weeping into
our lives

Our? What do you mean by that? Our . . .

All, Most, the people, the majority, the mass of beings

You believe in that?

Yes, that's what I do believe in. You don't

There's no proof there is anything real except myself, a class
if you like, and it's appetites.

Class? You admit there's a class then you admit to others.

No. Class is the body of the living entity, that inhabits all
of what exists except that tiny rat hole that you thrust your
nonsense out of. Only G can make a tree. But only I class can
make a G

Well done, over cooked, hard and rubbery like a burnt snake. You only. Class I you that with no them or any other.

Exactly. Do you sing? Or dance. Can you hum or drum. I've got use for what you ain't if you can be that as interest. Seven, eight, 10 percent The rest is appetite. Eating.

Tiny rat hole. Whoa. Don't you think that a little insulting. I don't even know you. Make yourself visible so I can spit on you. Or maybe hit you with an iron pipe. Or throw you down and stomp you in the chest,

I am visible. That's your defect, your manifest inferiority, that I can be seen but you don't see me.

Does that mean you're obscene?

In a way. Un scene is better the UN The Class The One The Theness of the not we nor us I ing . . . Check that

Could I pour food color where your voice is and see you then?

Try it!

Can I spray the blood of dead martyrs where your words hang momentarily and trace you that way?

Try that too

Suppose I got all the hungry people in the world to surround this spot where your talk comes from. Could I isolate you and waste you even without seeing you actually.

Can you do that?

I'll try

Look, don't waste your time. I admit it, I am G, I don't use drugs so I don't include the OD.

Don't use, just Sell

Exactly

What do you use?

Everything that's not me, to big myself into something lovable intelligent wise compassionate logical rational legal holy traditional innovative profitable

Do you consider your self Human?

NO, as I sd, I am G. There is no such thing as a Human.

Who am I?

A Bad Dream, continuing into the late afternoon.

Suppose I am not a Dream. Suppose I am Real. Suppose there are others. Suppose there are even Humans. Suppose you are a runt with a good cover story. Suppose you can be seen, and surrounded, and caught, and brought to trial. And Locked up. Or even executed?

You don't believe in the Death Penalty!

I would kill your voice, your ideas, your meaning, perhaps archive it with a photo of your notness to educate the others even if you never understood there are others.

Suppose everything I told you is a lie. And I am human, and a class and I know there are others. And that even you exist. But I like the way things are, except you being here taunting me with questions. Suppose suppose all that. Suppose, that everything you think and thought or will think about me is true. That I am somehow . . . what

Evil? Ugly? Ravenous? Greedy? Insane? A murderer? A Liar? A destroyer of Life and people. A kind of real devil. A Slavemaster? An Imperialist?

Now wait. Don't get carried away. So if I admit that I am a real thing, a class, and even most of those things . . . you say. . . . Slavemaster I can take . . . a Kind of Devil even, rest in piss, but an Imperialist. I don't use such language. I don't understand such language. I have 10,000 ignorant serial killer perderasts pumping what I need from all channels, stations, web sites, newspapers, schools, books, cds, and you want to resist with what? You don't have anything to fight me with but your tears, your whining, your empty frustration, your threat of humans and others . . . Bah

Are you up to challenges?

Oh . . . please I don't have all day. You still can't see me can you?

I want you to actually materialize. To be a real thing I can see, that I can point to and tell others, even if they don't exist, and even touch. I want you to do that, though you say it is all a fantasy, a bad dream, a rat hole perception. Still would you humor me and show your self in a way that would allow me the non-existent us to dig you, just for tough face glory?

You must be a nut and worse think I'm a nut.

Ok, you are a coward. But . . . let's do it this way. List all the things you hate!

Hmm- Everything that's not me, which therefore, could not exist

So you hate everything that can exist not being you?

Exactly

Well suppose I pull all that stuff that's not you that couldn't exist, suppose for my own rat hole humor I pulled all together, some way, if I could do that, would you help you.

Oh, well, just to stop this . . . of course, whatever you can do to pull together what is not me that does not exist that couldn't exist, I will help you do it. How?

Just by being even more you than you are now. Just by being gigantic you monster you incredibly everywhere appetite you . . . just by letting what does exist, all that, feel you more and more and somehow understand that they can't exist because only you and the rat hole could exist. Then what

OK, done, being done, will be done . . . and on . . . then what?

Well the rest is up to the rat hole, the non-existent others, the humans who never was, the rest is up to the can't be and wont be and wasn't. But then . . .

But then, Goodbye. . . . I'll be everywhere as usual. . . .

That's right And we'll see finally what is real and what aint and what that means

Hey, its been stimulating

At least, perhaps enlightening.

FASHION THIS, FROM THE IRONY OF THE WORLD.

That I, the undaunted Laureate of the place,
    daunted in some
Un as yet/ed pre tense of what they see, they be
As if, such where they was
Was yet to be, and then to say
They is, and is not, like revelations, wow!
Humans. The skin, the lodging inside dumbness a slight
    breeze frees they speech
To speak as if acquainted with small things in the world.
    Eating, Belching, Farting,
Murder, Robbery.
And so. As if, and them too they is. But nothing further
But the wee dots on the deletion resembling the minds of them
Yet to come.

Imagine you were me, or imagine you were thee
And we knew all the things both do. And is. And will ourselves
To be. Imagine you were in this place, and they wanted to run
    everywhere pointless
endless understanding not even why
They smell or they hair fall out, or what to do about
Gout. That they are yet stupid to colds and cancer and death—
    They think holy
And ultimate. When death is simply a report card

Of the ignorant. Nothing dies but that which never lived
And it might return in a white suit and in charge of ugly small
    mistakes
Somebody at Harvard could win a billion dollars and a post
If they cd find out but they never will because it is the reason
They committed suicide

Suppose you had to live with
Ignorant white people and negroes
In cages, with important chains
Around they mouths. Suppose you
Had heard of Trent Lott. Suppose, you woke up one am
And there was a vampire on the tube
Being interviewed by a Niggalino boob
A handsome rat, for whom the idea of brain
Was only an idea, which he did not think if he could
Was a bad one. And the boob was a killer yet to graduate
From killer school so he worshipped the vampire's teeth,
The two juicy fangs hanging from each end of his lip,
The negro thought was hip. And dreamed of having
Teefs like that so he could be a rat, he was tired of being
A mere heel. And the vampire was planning to bite the whole
World. To suck the blood out of everything. To suck the blood
Out of the world and make its future a vampire, that could
    whirl through

Space and suck the blood out of the stars, suck the blood out
    of the planets
Suck the blood out of the moon, suck the blood out of the sun
And then, armed and blubbery fat with everything's blood,
    still hot
And musical like emptiness, he could lift into the outer
    waygonesphere

And search for God, if there was such, and suck the blood out
of Him, Her, It, Them
Whatever, till there was no Blood anywhere, not even you,
Blood, in fact
You be one of the first to go.

It was a special issue of Jungle Comics, where the vampire the
thin nosed kind
From the out back, who can suck with his teef and stir with his
nose, who eyes
Are missing, and what you see is the bottom of a cold mine
filled with 2000 fathoms
Of Lynch, Execution, Missing, Rape, Cheated, Framed,
Slandered, Stolen, Frown
frozen ex corpuscles, hid under the glistening listening
underwater ASSCRAFT of
the Satanic moron cult, whose breath is toxic and pokes holes
in the sky so dead things
Can shit on our food.

He is called *Fonnghool the asshole,* and dances to dry lips set on
fire by missing
junkies he has eaten. He is the devil's newspaper and wears
his ass backwards so the colon can
Wear a uniform. And Revelations can be burned especially
18:12 where it say
beware of ugly mother fuckers who is not really ugly mother
fuckers but uglier
much, much, much more uglier dan dat! So spake Nat!
Amen. (

I speak with the rage of Angels
Them that be with Marx.

I speak with the clarity and inferno of the necessary
Like my man John on Patmos watching skyvision and
Digging it was all commercials.

I speak like Ali Baba, ("The Arabian Pope")
who when he spoke the magic words,
"Open this sucker up", and the mountain swang, envisioned
    one day
There would be a John named Trane who would blow the
    same shit

I blow with the deep fear of John on the island looking at the
    actual devil
I am like him in that I try to count the mammyjammers heads
    and horns
And find out what will kill him.

I speak like him who spoke to Philadelphia and hung out with
    Jesus
Before they murdered him. I speak like him who dug that Peter
Was a coward and gave the Lord up, and that Paul was an
    Anti-Semite
Who never came out the closet.

I speak as one who knew Judas would drop a dime on the
    Movement
And confirmed the chump had hung his lousy self just before
    I got busted.
I speak as one betrayed by the lies of those who say they are
    religious but
Are greed ridden worshippers of Satan, who kill any one who
    opposes them
and calls it a church of Defense against Evil.

Like John, I wd speak, like the John who baptized, like John
the knower, John,
The Blower. John the Brown and John The Revelator. I speak
like James the
Brother, James the other, Jim the hip, like Dick the Rude, like
Bird the high, like
Monk the Deep I speak from the island of my soul, and cast a
terrified look into the
sky filled with monsters, with witches and devils with Great
Whores and Beasts, of
things with heads and horns and blood dripping out of their
eyes.

It is *out,* imagine, you were here, in this place, staring into the
soul of something
Filthy, trying to keep it from murdering you, to keep your
eyes from registering
Your ears from hearing, your mouth from reporting. And you
could feel it
breathing on your neck and saw sometimes the shadow of its
horny hands reaching out of the
Blind dark you cd see the shadow of its gun its lie its teeth
sweating. Imagine you
could actually understand its obscene ideas, and they made
you enter the mind of
Fred Douglass And stare out at the ocean just as John at the
edge of Africa, staring at the
Overhead commercials on the death of the Beast.

And so the blessing that is in my name and in my words, I give
to myself
And you who are truthful as the actual life of the world. And
it is this blessing

Which will save us, will make us strong, as we go on with our
    work of scientifically
Determining how to kill the beast. Each night I fill my
    notebooks with formula
And instructions to myself and others on what to do of what
    to study of where to
Go who to talk to and when. I make lists of words, names,
    events, processes,
necessary stages of what we have come to realize is protracted.
    And what we do we will do.
And what we succeed at, is worth the pain, what we fail at, is
    worth the
understanding if we can understand. What the next step is.
    We are studying with all
our minds and hearts and souls' determination to understand
    how to slay the serpent. This task
Nat handed down to whoever did understand that that was
    what he did, hanging on
That tree. Slain by the Serpent's hosts.

So we have learned that we can not die except by our own
    submission to it.
And have decided we will not die except when we understand
    what place we go to.
And so begin to set that where in order and begin to
    understand where the beast
Will be hiding there. We are the Rider of The Black Horse.
    Black Horse Black
Rider, who conquers with a scale. With Justice and Measure
    and the mighty
pentatonic mode of the finite music of infinity, a new joint . . .

And when I returned from this forwarding of my feeling and
   knowing
The beast sat still and teeth wiggled with lies and at once I
   remembered where
Before I'd seen him, before his tenure as the Counterfeit Ghost
of The Caucasian Crib. Yes, it was the same one. Remember
   the little

Devil Gerald 2X arrested and placed in the pages of
   Muhammad Speaks
And we saw him where Malcolm had locked him up, with the
   little
Horns out his head the evil eyes and the twin fang straws for
   sucking oil and blood.

It got clear to me as he rose to leave, and the negro boob
   slobbered happiness
At being recognized as the newest commode in the Caucasian
   abode, the vampire
Turned and where before the cunning little tail that used to
   dangle out his hiney
Struck me at its absence, Oh, I thought, and at that moment I
   saw the thing dart
Like a copper head's fart out of the negroes curled lips,
   ringed with the white chalk
Caucasian Circle of Merit which identifies Wooden Negroes
   promoted to the
honorary genus of *Homo Locus Subsidere* (literally, "Near
   Man"), who no longer
kneel when they are made well paid heels, but now can
   assume the funky bedbug crouch of the
Hideously self hating. At the same time, they are given a grey
   facsimile carte blanche

Weapon of Ugliness to use against N words and any who wd
    violate the sanctity
Of northern appetite! And so I came to understand that the
    beast's deadly arrow,
Shot from out the 1st horseman's white bow, from the white
    horse, the weapon
which Revelations prophesied to John, was the weapon of his
    transitory rule, was now
The tongue of the boob, whom I err at calling him that, or
    rat, or heel, or dog, or
Traitor. That tail become a tongue was the sign, that from the
    vampire's tail
Was bestowed on the wooden negro a badge that allowed him
    to enter Klan meetings,
Skin Head Lynchings, Texas Executions, Palestinian Ethnic
    Cleansings, and report
With the slobber of his terrificatious white ringed serpents
    beak, symbol, font &
punctuation on the tabula rasa of the media sheet the empty
    echo of his eviscerated
Self, and in the soul's place that beast's tail was hung that
    beast's tale was sung.
And I stood, remembering Patmos, and the images that sailed
    across the air
When you and I was there. And wondered what next the
    world of this life held for those
Who would love goodness.

HOLE NOTES

It is an ugly game they ain't
Playing. Like a tree cd walk away
Singing, it got a band of rocks
& snakes & dizzy flies.

Is a ugly dream they telling
& make the silence bleed
& winter cringe in bed
a crimson balloon carrying
the words, is that a
crocodile, where they come
any thing ain't dead be
numb. A bird sit here
a panic color beak
a midget flower weeping
a sun afraid to wholly shine
so it eyelid a beam not to
out do the insolent whatever
of grey dirty tragicness. A frog
talking shit & a monkey
translate it into media hit.
A dog, go way, say through
The telephone. Call the Zoo for
Appointments. A weasel w

A briefcase staring at us.
A worm with a good gig
Now he come laughing at both of us
A possum telling jokes.

A path is not pathing.
A well is ill.
A river refuse wetness.

Night in the wings picketing
Earliness & storms in its
Eyes gibbering the news]
of idiots getting rich
Again getting saved
Again being born
Again. Amen. A shark
Has a house next to the
Where you want to go

A below a sideways
An alley clings to the garden
Owning your alternatives
Why do you want to
Be here broke
Spring won't appear
Afraid of winter here
Everybody refuses to
Acknowledge their everyness
& leave their body outside
who nature question is dirty

I Am Sent Photographs of My Aunt Georgia's 90th Birthday Party in South Carolina

They don't know they

Horrible. How could they. To look, at, like that, that woman
who was once

So full of breath, the sun, life, to me

That winter I was undesirably discharged

From America. Oh Say Can you, Jezzus H. Christ, Ya fuckin –A-

Tweety, inside me, in the world, out on the dim grim distant
howling, summer

feeling wood houses

Of South Carolina. A little boy casts his being up through the
menace of being that.

Here

The snake oil volcano killer. Nigger slaver. Undesirable, you
bet.

Then to bare all that as far as it had riz, in him, to her, to find
out

Some bit of who it meant

He was, would be. No, they don't

They didn't NO. How could they

Disarm the memory of that wonderful knowing (except the
trial she bore

Of a stupid negro vodka weening clumsy androgynous
message from

The white house, "We dig yall can be tilted toward the
    badness we acknowledge,
and give you . . .)
Like Silas Marner in High, yeh? School, the dark crowding up
    around his face,
As he sat drunk, not, near, yeh, babbling about what ever he
    didn't
Understand.
Georgia, Georgia, on my life, old slender, tall, straight, half-a-
    laughing Auntie
Mine. There now, with negroes groveling for meaning, no,
    crawling out of
themselves, back in themselves
For feeling, not. The corniest things in the world
Are boring.

They couldn't, all that time. Her fate was to be
Ironic, in the midst of that. At herself. At them. The world.
    That's why
She talked so fast! That softly sharping
"titter" that held the world somewhere, beyond arm's length.
    Near the moon
of whatever was her deep desire. Yet to be there, in that, and
    expecting it to
desire her, as she, half consciously accepted what it was
and the limitations to her streamlined rocket feeling self. Oh
    Jezus, Jezus,
Jeeeezszus
H. Christ. And
that little boy looked into her face, and she into his, and what
    they didn't
understand of each other
was what they loved most.

But not this. Not this contemptuous disgust with life,
The bookend Negro believes is love, my Jesus lord, not that,
Or devotion. Please. No, don't say that. Or
Celebration, of a life
They never, no they didn't, don't you understand? They
Never understood.

So they send me these horrible pictures, and what do they
    expect from me?
except to be right
again. They always are, but not about anything
that matters.

Georgia, Georgia, The Whole night through
Just an old sweet song
Keeps Georgia
On my mind.

Farewell sweet Auntie.

The Terrorism of Abstraction

Why disappear & lie
    we can see you
        why cover everything
            w/ the sad victory
                of silence?

    Why pretend to see
And only advertise blindness. Why
  Claim a tongue, ears, a
      Mouth & instead produce
          A tiny heart too jittery
             To beat. Why costume
                Feeling with bone shine
             & shallow glitter?

Why lie an "I" & vanish
Into parsed diction. Why
Enhance an empty place
With fantasy furniture
& say it is the truth?

Why not tell us something
Other than the sound effects
Of impotent evasion?

Why make believe poetry
Is about arrogant pretense
& social denial. Why
try to trick us you can sing?

Why make words dull
to conceal passive
submission to
Weak regret?

No Voice, Don't Go, Don't Go, Voice on a Screen It Still Seem Real, Yet You Know It's Really Gone w/

OUR MAN, PEDRO. The dark streak of this into that
The Jones that came with his laugh, The Zorro hat, every body
Shda knowd, Pedro. But, how cd they
With poison Bush in our nose, they cdnt shdnt didn't know
Pedro. Some say he split, like re loaded he rose, in a plane
so he cd go without the used up wings of myth or mister ology.
And with him, with Pedro. Mustache, Si, the sloping always up
     roared eyes.
The walk, the medals, for the bravery and courage to make war
On yr outrage, oh midgets of stupidity. Pedro laughs at you,
     and we too because of him Laugh at you and his
box "loose joints"
Laugh at you in the telephone booths of replaced American
     hearts, from inside them Pedro makes the telephone
booths laugh at you, The rubbers he threw
At you in the Negro lady's house laugh too. And the dead
     Hermanos y Hermanas laugh at you, even "without
     underwears".
So, why aint he here?
How come he and Mikey, Vincent, Nina, went away? Who book
They so. We can't live without Pedro in black
Giving corny people heart attack. How can it be?
We left with out he? Pedro, El Bandito del Poesia
El Zorro del Loisaida. The Nuyorican Beacon.

El Reverendo Palante. Sermon *Obit,* some heavy shit. How the
Mice was goin' to parties and the bloods, Los Pueblo
Tienen no Vida al todos. From mice to Rat
The Dead Uniform let the Swine know where
They at . . . There was no other being brought them Ricans
    here
Where we cd see and hear they lives.
The *Obit* made it clear.
Juan, Miguel, Milagros,
Olga, Manuel,
buried in
the empty box of Americans'
missing soul.

That was the passport called "Yo Tengo Puerto Rico En Mi
    Corazon".
That same church Felipe stood up in, where the Lords declared
We were blood and kin. So then we have to see Pedro lying
    there
Playin' us like he sleep, when we know
in a minute he gonna start running them telephone booth
    poems
Its gon' be deep.
        But did anybody laugh till they bend and weep.
Anybody wake up baiting the darkness with disorder.
    Reversing the tied,
So an ocean of Ha Ha's turn us into waves of its rush.
Who cd lose that and be the same, or stay sane, or find they
    brain.
Pedro gotta be with us, he Deeper and funnier than El Senor.
Pedro who walks sideways without moving
Whose words were champion story tellers, who never lied,
and told the truth on the installment plan.
Whose shoes made him sing.

Who jump start us with crack-up Vision,
whose tunnel of mouth, Ha Ha Ha'd serious incision.

That voice, that Latin Insomniac, Reverendo, black glove,
    razor sharp
possessed perception must always be with us,
that weapon
of refusal to be locked down in the dull squalid mortuary of
    frowns
of white frozen overhead toxic deadly
America. Who lied to say we arrived, and all we see is slaves
In the box car of history's cold leftovers.
That's why Pedro wore them medals
And gave the Puerto Rican passport to people made illegal aliens
By they mind.
Nothing can ever sound like Pedro at full blessed laugh.
Nothing can bop they head up and down
So the words mortar-shell across us screaming that revelation.
Mix us together, Oh, Co-mix. Like The Djali sposed to do.
Oh dark Taino Hermano of the stalking
Guanguanco walk. The mystery shadow cover of meaning
behind which he is coming while going,
encircling the world with the machine gun of his words.
A thousand suns a minute Bang Bang the night and day of
    this that
into the force of Si, Aye, Eye, Yes and Of Course and Certainly
    and Yeh,
and Amen Amen Amen.
With that open embrace Elegba, Osiris, Orpheus, thus Djali,
    now Djali ya,
Out of the darkness, his passion ultra-violet booms purple
    alphabets
        & split the night world into indigo lips
as he blue blew the first sun rise and the first dawn

467

whose chromatic ascension is the key board of human boom
    a looms

So if he gone, he must come back nobody wanna live where it
    always night
The voice and walk, and mustache, and eyes, and that raging
    live for what it is,
es Verdad es Hermosa, nobody cant remove that day
it lay in the box plotting
Under that same hat the next sun's laughing.
              So sit here with me
                in the other room
after the church, the mud and snow and tears of the Bronx
    cemetery,
                after the worried highway of hello goodbye
    hugs kisses quiet cryings, after the flick, old friends,
the beer wine rum Jack Daniels, hard smiles forced into
    sound, when the Nuyorican close down, this night
with our sadness, at that bottom of ourselves
where the silence has muscles.

In a minute you will hear light,
and see words flowing out of darkness
like rich blue wine, and there will come that voice, the hat,
    that mustache
and grinning ironic eyes, see, Si!

Well what did you expect,
the darkness fades away and there is the day
with loose joints hanging from the sun burning with light
Of course, it's Elegba, Osiris, Orpheus, The Glee Man, back at
    they gig
Then Everybody scream, "Hey Pedro, Man Where you been?"

468

WHOOSH!

After The Rain

I used to be simple
    When the world
        Was

"When was that"?
An LP after the '45
After the '78
When the sky was far away
When humans had faces
When the world minded
    Its own business
    & poetry was a dream
    that left no foot prints

I used to be ignorant
    & thought I cd live
    without killing

I used to be quiet
I used to look at things
& wonder
that was before
    the war
    before the other

war & the war
before
that.

I used to be a child
I got outta that
I used to be excited
    By what I didn't
        Understand
I was still a child then
    Not yet a man

I used to think I cd do anything
    But stuff I didn't wanna
        Do

I thought every body
    Had a heart, a soul,
    A brain, was sane

I don't mean some of what
    I saw & knew, & passed
    Wasn't mean. But
    It didn't mean
    What Monk mean
    When he thought up
    "I Mean You!"

I never wanted to be anything
But everything good. I thought
I understood good. Like an appetite
I might have, a beautiful feeling,
A sound, a little girl her hair

In a little curl, rolled
Like an instant on her
Forehead.

    I used to think
      Dead people
        wd always
            be dead.

    And you saw them
      If you had to
          just a moment
          at funerals.

    I stopped that
    I wont look at
        The funeral dead
        But instead I find the
    Dead, behind, to the left
        the right,
           & Straight ahead

There's a Dead thing
    With a pretzel
        Stuck in his cheek
A ghost w/o a Sheet
A murderer with an Ant Eater's
Beak. An ex-cartoon character
In *Muhammad Speaks*
      w/ pointy ears, 2 Lugosi teefs
stick out his ant eater mouf
      you lookin' for that

cute little tail
    he had

When Gerald 2x
Created him like Jacoub
& Malcolm kept him
    jailed inside
The Black Muslim
    Newspaper.

I used to laugh at that
    Little devil, years after
    One told me
        Harlem smelled like
        The Elephant House
          at Bronx Zoo
          and I knew
          like he knew
          that he was
          tryin' to hurt
          me.

I used to cry
if I had
    to lie.

I used to think
    Every thing was its own
    Solution. That people
    Who put Colored People down
    Were just crazy. I don't think
    I understood their power.

I thought that Negroes
Who "cut the fool"
Were like a mysterious odor
From a garbage can.

I don't think I ever really
    Believed in God
I got baptized
      & nothing happened
      except I got wet
      & blinked my eyes
      at a preacher whiter
      than white people
      so I guess I thought
      he cd protect us
      from evil

All this time
    In my zig zag
      Growing

All this looking & feeling
    & eventually
      knowing

Both me and the
    World
    Dig changing

I used to be
    & so forth
      me & the

world
　　says
　　　cd say
　　　　did say
　　　　will say

I used to, used to
　　How did that word
　　　　Come to mean that?

SPEAK TO ME THROUGH YOUR MOUTH

Speak to me through your mouth
Not the Daily Noose or Santa Claus fake animals
I see on television. Speak to me in my ears. Loud enough
For me to hear. Tell me what is the matter with us, why
We are sitting here being directed to Hell by Ugly greedy
Lying Zapalote, who claim you love them, that's why they must
Kill us. Talk to me out of your own brain not the box of idiots
Whose eyes send odors through the tube, who have mastered
        the art
Of telling the Beast where we live, so we can wake up grinning
Tell me, look at me while you speak. Touch me to make sure
        we're both here.
Ask me a question and I'll ask you one.
Can we conversate for a minute
Promise you won't call me an egotistical dribble of unlikely
        desire.
I won't call you out your name. Call me through the windows
        of the evening.
Can you sing? Then do that. A song we both know. What about
        the *Internationale?*
You never heard of it?
You want to sing *Past Time Paradise?* You're not Stevie Wonder,
        Are you?

Are you a friend or an enemy? My friend or my enemy. I'm a
poet. I
carry a RAZOR in my vest. You know Langston Hughes. You love
Aimé Césaire. You can't
Play baseball, but you can box. You have on blue. You are
covered
everywhere with blue. Your eyes are indigo, are you a woman
or a man.
Why didn't I ask you before?
Before what? Is the door open to your heart? Can your lips
play music?
Are your fingers somewhere close? Do I know you? Have we
ever met?
How did you get there?
I'm here where I am for a long time. The window loves me.
How can I
see you? You don't care to see me? Why not? Ok, but still,
speak to me
through your mouth.
I hope you're not a priest or a detective.

John Island Whisper

I thinking cost you a window sees you
In the sky of our limit is, our unsung unacknowledged
Nation. O want us we being free we, like
A star we staring, unseen and street is caring
Want to know and do, and be that
If we to, like singing so beautiful
Blood is true. I wish, they say. And we wishes. Wishes
Too. Is them a god, they tell us
Is. No we ain't but that which is
Here and talked to
Gesture stupid. Am arm clock faceless breath a song nobody
    know and
we the words and the melody. Say it hymn ain't singing them
Is there singable me and you too. A singable love. A warm
    tune-ish be
for us That eyes can hear the lowering happy the sun inside
Be the overhead living

Alas, Poor Auden, I Knew Him,

A poet fiend of mine dropped this on me /// At a DC poetry soiree recently
during the polemics on art & or VS politics, one disingenous ungenius
quoted Auden to maintain that his work finally was just a tidier way of
"wacking his doodle". Yo boy's reaction to dat follows.

The Tragedy of Taste
    I would have sd to Auden,
Reading the wasted tragedy of his repulsion
from his own courage. How we can be backed up
from love by the anonymous hatred rising off
the streets like mist off the terra of the flat
foolishness of wishing God did not exist under-
standing He don't Sayin he ain't , then copping to
The lie of your own dishonesty in the face of
the fists of Ignorance which mock us con-
cretely with windows and elevators.

    Poor Auden, to escape the Red Paint, he wd
mumble "Poetry does nothing . . ."
When, at least, it got him in trouble.
Like the rest of us, willing to fight ugly, cuss
ugly, smack ugly in its face, or talk bad to it
in our house, or at some forgotten bar, where
our spit rolled down the face of a denying
grey flannel racist heart.

    Poor Auden, living a lie, his crying, his backed
in the corner punkishness, as legacy and
not at least, the sophistication of pre-

Enlistment into "The Horror", like
Brando in the sunken hills and bleeding caves
of inferno Viet-Nam
Tricked by ego into joining The Monsters
who let themselves be slaughtered to
honor the prophecy of Revelations.

Poor Auden, Remember how he sd of the search
for fire, for the self-consciousness of coming humanity
How he constumed its failure in his mind as
The Greeks, wrapped in the tragedy of
their own self predictions, a man "falling
out the sky", somehowing us that we
could never discover the wisdom of our
own being, subtracting our future with
their icy truncations.
Alas, to slay one's father, push up on they own
Mother, then on top of that
cut they own eyes out so they could get outta
Europe, head for the U.S. and make a deal
with some African Negroes to buy slaves.

Poor Auden, "Poetry Does Nothing", He wept,
closed in near Birdland, waiting for
Pee Wee Marquette.

Poor Auden, Finally to show up on the
Lower East Side, closeted with Chester K.
Winking at Frankie O & the others, whis-
pered about, his betrayals become a robe
of curiosity for those not yet bloodied by
their own denials.

"I sold out, Ok, I sold out!" A dude I knew,
the newspapers called "A Genius" at 20,
Thirty years later, He kneels
in the hotel lobby, asking some Black poet
to "forgive him", for getting rich and having three houses,
one in the Indian Territory. "Forgve me, Please!" He said.

Ask, Auden, Poor Auden. What poetry does
is leave you when you stop needing it!.

At a funeral, a man I knew,
A mysterious blonde, resourceful as the movies,
as consort of the famous & glamorous
wearing that like a toga of sunshine indoors.
Alas, Auden, could be blanched, tho reddened, by the question,
'What are you doing?" A friend from his history in exile,
'Writing soap operas" twists into
what bitter sophistication sells as smile . . .

"The Young & The Restless"

"Oh, Yeh!" the skinny history, in that still youthful
anxiousness his casual watchers cannot see, Laughing,
"Hey, man, how much they paying you?"
It was no guile or mischief in that query, only another bit of
information to
give a base to any theory.

But the glamorous blonde of now
was daunted deep somehow, and with the chortle
of quick steps out the back door of his
feelings, sd, "Don't ask me, It's obscene!"

Indeed, in a word, two syllables, Poor Auden.
To leave a disgusting lie as signature
A simple forgery in place of his soul
Auden, Poor Guy, like himself at that bar half-drunk
and sunk with half digust, for those who would not give up
the Sweet filth of Sodom
who'd rather be covered in that silken gore
As glorified whore
There, and likewise lauded
in Gomorrah, like Weldon's intelligent Darky
Preferring disguise and a crown of lies
Wanting himself seen only through a glass
Darkly.

As in, Poor Auden
Poor Poor Auden.

Nightmare Bush'it Whirl

Full of fiends, friends dyin'
Why we cryin, was a zoomy yesterday power in they very
    sound,
& the laughter & wild crying, they fightin', keep tryin', we
    usta know
we was stronger than the devil insect brain. But teeth whirl,
    eat ya. Eat us. Whip
whirl, hide under yr feets, bitin' on top and underneath.
    Crazy stomping gurgle us
world. Cd catch up. Malcolm. Could trap. Lumumba. Could
    dive down and beat,
Biko. Could lie and Use stink from his very ass to kill, Toure,
    Nkrumah, Cd bite
inside yellow pages
Huntin' for unemployed maniacs. Sibeko. Cd speak
    Portuguese
Send poison fleas, Cabral. Cd white out mouth
And sneak in as dressed up nothing, King. Cd yesterday
    themselves in afterwards
the oh ohhs of hyena ghosts
Crawling out dunce hats as the furniture polish of Watergate
    killers. Mao. Cd be
wasted by the insanity of mistakes and
The magnifiers of greenmail unrighteous left us prey. Stalin.
    Cd be lied about

Or ignored, misused like diarrhea, clouding the world to a
    ho's toilet, Lenin.
Cd be studied to death in dust swept clean oh Marx Engels
Under the academic Preyer rugs of

Loyal opposition bedbugs, right, Mayakovsky, cd be olded
By the torture of escaped assassination attempts, murders.
    "You know we shd'a
killed you. You shd'a stayed w/ Fidel or
The Chinese, Rob Wms. Where's yr Negro gun now, the Ku
    Klux Klan in the white
house, Dr., & Garvey didn't send them there, Rabin dead in
    his own Jewish state
Some of his own folks did the hate. Yitzak.
Why this the whole ugly we have to eat or beat or flee or don't
    see or disclaim we
know its name
Or be happy but insane. Was we always drugged and dead,
    Huey. Was we
Always fat and fulla shit, OH Elephant? Was we always
    Crouched or
midget Booker T's hoping they cd intermarry silence in the
    20th century.
Was we always nostalgic failures
Unable to sleep even when awake. Was we only Donald Duck
    opponents
Of the mouth, in black beret dashikis, reappearing
As baldhead charlatans in Rolls Royces, hot with the
    demagoguery
Of deluded obsession? Was we always drop outs from the cp
    who turn up as Black nationalists

Because we didn't have no real childhood? Was we always
    bought and sold like
cheap candy. Didn't we never stand up straight or was we
Even before the world split open and the frown sat over our
    head like heavy weather
Walking in a crouch, to be near the man
Who hadn't even come out Jacoub's test tube yet?
Wes we always cannibals and scalpers like the white people
    really was
Was we always the Remus who mama was a wolf and brother
In the snow. Slay what. What you say. Ain't gon' be like this oh
    president named
after a reefer, oh serial killer of
The of revelation doom channel, watch the end. Where the
    beast get popped and the
white horse white rider
Be stopped, and Red Ryder and the Indian, make war with
    history

                                Wait'in on the beboppers to arrive
                                      Eatin' fish sammiches
                                    And talking the smack of
                                              Hard fact

                                              Won't be no act
No it wan be, can't be like that, in history and now be the
    future befo' you change
Them nasty cash register drawers.

Say I ain't dreaming, this just ain't screaming, what I say, what
    you say,
Is this real or not, the beast got to be dropped
A tombstone raise over his stink

Say this backward dog thought he was God
& dead is where his ugly led, he was much more evil
than the future think, and got to be a cd inside the stone
that holler out to all who approach
You might still have some problems
but none of em bad as the ghost!

A World!

PROCERT

In the dark unlicensed room
The fear of light waylaid any thing except
The people who didn't know where anything was.
They could whisper anything, to anything, but could not sing.

Instead, the bled head, and the lies yet to be
Said, collided inside the panorama of future amazement.
    They had seen
The television, read the New York Times, listened to madmen
    and fools
And wanted to laugh, if they had lips. So they sat under
    themselves and
Tried to understand weeping.

This was not Ramadan, or Christmas, or Yom Kippur, or The
    wooden jelly
Bells of the old plantation when your relatives was there,
    considering murder.

And Lo, that's what they were, then, to them, and when that
    passed, they sat up
Gasped a few notes that the critics, Shaitan bless'em, called
    "Rag". And so passed into

The great millennium of Nina Simone, singing, "Oh, Lord,
Don't let me be misunderstood!"

The darkness wedged itself inside the colorless person's
    throat, and when he sang
It rang, bang-awang-gang. And silently, like truth, some youth
    put on different
colors and made old people mad for having to feel like that
    all the time.

The unsaid mischief of blue street dimly lit, where the
    footsteps hung
So no one would mistake what they couldn't see for what had
    never been.

A lady like a magazine Bird, costumed in colors that whistled
    and stomped, preyed
on the disarranged minds, a Wooly bully teeth & stomach
    smiled like weather
reports and said stupid shit to confirm he was as important as
    the unswept floor of
the colored church where everybody had to be happy because
    God was watching.

You say, "I wanna Cry, but don't let me die, cause I won't lie,
    etcetera, smash." No
cataclysm except the bubbles.
No crucifixion, except we had been lied to.

"Let us know when we can sing", you sd.
"Nothing complex, like the Jelly Glass concertos, writ last
    semester when smiling
was accepted."

So now in the same gloomish castle of unfettered conceit, where some Negroes won't
    even eat meat, and others
Have no teeth, and some more, got a cross they bore, and
    more than them, includes
me and you, Jim.

In that wrestled downpour of sudden silence, the lights pitter
    twinklings of dim
regard. And lost people whine
They have received no reward, and the logarithms of justice
    are unsolved
And hide in wrinkled documents otherwise stuffed with lies
And nobody got on a bathing suit or pilot goggles, and the
    statues
Won't move, since they too old, like Kenny G, to go to Iraq
With "The Natives". And the policemen won't hold a decent
    conversation
Before they pull the trigger. Bang Bang Bang, etcetera.

Just a sliver of light, an innocent song, would save us. But alas,
    is that all
In the past, with Movie heroes and the United States?

Arafat Was Murdered!

I KNOW WE KNOW
THEY KILLED ARAFAT
THEY MURDERED HIM
I KNOW YOU KNOW
WE KNOW THEY KNOW
THEY MURDERED HIM
THE ISRAELIS AND AMERICANS
THEY MURDERED ARAFAT.
BUT NOT THEM ALONE
THOUGH THEY ARE THE BEASTS
FROM THE WEST & THE EAST
THERE WERE OTHERS, CLOSER,
MUCH CLOSER, INSIDE HIS
PLACE, LOOK FOR THE TRACE
WE WILL FIND IT, WE ARE NOT
BLINDED & WE KNOW, I KNOW
YOU KNOW, ARAFAT WAS
MURDERED. AS SURE AS
SHARON IS UGLY & BUSH
A SWINE, THEY PICKED
THE TIME, WHEN THE
NORTH AMERICAN SLIME
WERE STEALING THE
ELECTION, WHEN MOST

WERE HYPNOTIZED BY
OPENED THE DOOR,
SOME WHORE, SO THE
BEAST CD ENTER & MURDER
OUR FRIEND, ASSASSINATE
YET ANOTHER PEOPLES'
LEADER, SO THEIR GREED
COULD BITE & CHEW
& SWALLOW & DIGEST
& TURN OUR LIVES
INTO FECES. I KNOW YOU
KNOW IT WAS NOT JUST
BUSH & SHARON, THEY CDN'T
DO IT ALONE, THERE WERE
OTHERS, CLAIMING TO BE
SISTERS & BROTHERS, WE
MUST SEEK THESE UNKNOWN
BEASTS, THE LITTLE SWINE
WHO MAKE US STUMBLE
THE LICE WHO LIVE
ON THE DOG'S DIRTY
SKIN, WHO MAKE NOISES
LIKE COMRADES & FRIENDS
WHO SUCK ON THE BONES
TOSSED BY BUSH & SHARON
WHO ARE KNOWN SWINE
DOG MONSTER BEAST
MURDERERS, WE KNOW
YOU WILL TELL WHY
SO MANY OF US DIE,
AND WHY BUSH & SHARON
DENY & FOX & MICKEY
MOUSE LIE, &

THE CHILDREN OF THE
OPPRESSED GO HUNGRY
& CRY. TELL THE
WORLD ABOUT PALESTINE
& WHO COMMITTED
THE CRIME, TELL THEM
WHO KILLED OUR COMRADE
YASIR ARAFAT, TELL
THEM, EXPLAIN, EXPOSE
THE INSANE, THE SAME
MANIACS THAT KILLED
YITZAK RABIN,
THE SAME SHADOWY FIEND
HAS STRUCK ONCE AGAIN
YES, BUSH & SHARON
ARE THE KILLERS WE KNOW
BUT IN THE SHADOW
VERY CLOSE, TERMITES
& WORMS, GUSANOS
666 INTERNS

DAY FRIENDS
NIGHT FRIENDS

FOR WHOM PALESTINE
IS SOMETHING
ONLY TO BE
SAID, & WHO
ARE POISONS TO
MAKE CERTAIN OUR
PEOPLE AND LEADERS
GET DEAD

I KNOW AT LEAST
WE CAN DO THAT

TO SCREAM AT THE

TOP OF OUR VOICES

WE KNOW THEY
    MURDERED
        OUR FRIEND

YASIR ARAFAT!

LOWCOUP

No one can be more full of
      Shit
    than those who claim
    to speak
        for God!

Silent Night

    Whenever the Devil
    Is disguised
          As God
    He is called
          Santa Claus!

Lowcoup Lingusitic

for Chu The

in Mandarin,
   The word
      BUSH

   Mean

   DUMB

   MOTHER FUCKER

Mr. Personality

Every time I see him
      He's going Nowhere
         & he just
            got back

Hold On, I'm Coming

The Church finds
Same Sex Marriage
Vile
Yet they are full of
Pedophiles
It's Not Homosexuality
They oppose
They just don't wanna
Get married!

FOR BUSH 2

The Main Thing
   Wrong
      w/ You
  is
      You ain't
  in
  Jail

The Devil Issues a Press Release

Now that the
White Boy
Got
More Power
than God
He wanna come
Fuck
wit me!

Progressive Nazi

Bush is more democratic
        Than Hitler,
He made Eva Braun
        Secretary of State.

Craziness

Is no act
  Not to act
Is crazinezzzz

Low Couphorism

Nothing unusual
    Has Ever
        Happened—

And "Ever"
        Is Meta-
            Physical.

Religious Note

Only Heathens
Would call
The Friday
Before Easter
"Good"!

Famous Doo Doo

When you become
Immortal
They pack you in
Stone
& Let birds
Shit on your
Head

Nay Toe

Yo!
If Jack
The ripper
Had a gang
It wd be called
  NATO!

Now What?

Imagine, no understand,
Shit has a brain
And a God!

BIG FOOT

Shaw Nuff

If you ever saw Bird talking to
Billy Shaw, about business, about
pleasure, about cops and copping, or about anything
You'd probably recognize Bird, that abstract expressionist
Vine he always had on, Black stripes, Yellow stripes, No stripes
Yet Bird never went to jail. A bunch of his running buddies,
    sycophants
and dearest friends did, trying to be Like Bird. Trying to play
    that music.
Because the music was Bird. It would come out of that
    glittering Ax
and sail up through the top of the sky and carry all the
    diggers with it.
So alot of people thought it was in them Yardish Ko Ko bags,
    or mixed up
inside the stash, dropped in with the Skag and Vonce and
    Dooji and Mud.
So a buncha mammy jammers mumbled the victrola needle
    into a poison spike.
Even Bird, one night, at Birdland, was jabbing the flagpole
    deep into his vein
and Dizzy peeped when the door flang open. And you know
    what Dizzy said,

"Hey, that motherfucker in there shooting up!"
The shit and the works leaped out of Bird's mitts, and everything hit
with a Zildjan bamalama Clang. And Bird, drugged and double drugged
leaped next, up off the toilet seat, and out into the smoky crowd, careful
as he split, not to run into the little "half a mammy jammer" Pres had named
Entering the outside of Birdland, half high, embarrassed like BA his tail smoking
but still grounded, down here fleeing the wouldbe alchemists of what it was.
When they caught up with him, after America had burned to the ground, Bird
was still warm. But as he explained, "I just did all that shit, to show you what not
to do! You dig?" A few did.

Confirmation

     This song will always be about Love
for me. Bird knew, and told you too, when he played
and the hip things stayed right inside your knot
surrounding you at the same time, with the worlds future
when human beings had finally copped. But then when the music
stopped, and Bird became Charlie Parker, and the bright light of his
Seeing was silent like Bach waiting for Be Bop, there was still Bird
inside his knot, Confirming the Beauty of what is Beautiful and the

distance ugliness was flung, by the frantic beat of a heart on
    fire with
another hearts touching, His eyes seemed to whirl in slow
    funkishness
seeing us and what was beyond us trying to explain.
As weird as it is, Love is a form of knowledge, and any persons
    you say you love know
you like you know them. My wife, Amina, is like that, for me,
    the heartbeat, like my
own, and what it is is what it says and what it reaches is what it
    touches.
Love is weird, like I say. It aint always still and humming,
    sometimes, like Bird
its wants to wail and cant. And some other times, you feel it
    flying above you
screaming how much it loves you. Yeh, It's out.

    Buzzy

      was the obscene parable of my vanishing adolescence.
    You better get
away from you because you always know what you think. You
    better get further
and smell better. You better not ride the buzzard's back, he'll
    take you somewhere
you cant get back. All them betters, used to play me like Ol
    man mose under the
piano bench trying to cop what the others could not. And so I
    took it as other
everything I heard from my father and mother. That it was,
    the word, like I had
already heard Bird. Repetition was my introduction to face to
    face blood to blood

profundity, psychological profanity and well advertised
  insanity. It was Charlie
Parker, talking bout . . . "you better get yrself
          ." Oh, no, I will not say those sad words again.
  Whistling in the Hall
like I would always be in college, every Fall. But Bird, I heard,
  when I had left the
crib of my own distancing, and embraced my out as not the in
  it had been and the
the rest of my feeling was not in concealing what I knew or
  wanted. And I was a real
person, who bled and hurt, who didn't inderstand a lot of
  things I needed to. When
I copped, that dead Saturday of ancient heartbeat, the fact
  that it is the world that is
in you and you in it. When I dug, that I must learn who I was
  by learning what the
world was. . . . my blue insides spread like a thin glowing song
  all in front of me and my
hands sparkled with what they knew they would do, whenever.
  Then I turned
and walked back into my yet to be discovered life. A hip
  nigger kid, brighter than
all the lights at Chanute Air Base and several ugly cities. And I
  felt myself leap
and begin to experiment with flight. That night, it was in
  Chicago, I touched myself
and felt myself and my head emptied and began to fill at the
  same time. And Buzzy,
why he was off somewhere, tragically expiring in some ugly
  woman's pad. And I,
I'll confess, wasn't even sad. But I have been, often, since
  then. And this poem, makes
me sad again.

Four Cats on REPATRIATIONOLOGY

Dude asked Monk
If he was interested
In digging
   The Mother
         Land

Monk say,
"I was in the
Motherfuckin
      Mother Land
      before

       & some mother
                   fucka

brought me
over here

   to play
    the
   mother
           fuckin
  piano. . . .

   You, dig?"

A.#
Another Dude
 Asked Duke
the same question

Was he, "interested
In Digging
The Mother
Land?"
Duke say, "Yeh

      I go there

Every evening!"

B♭

   Same Blood
   Hit on Miles
                   Like that
   "Say Miles
   You wanna go to

The Mother
Land?"

"Yeh, tell her
To call me!"

C.

Same Dude ask
        Louis
          About Return

        To the Mother Land

          "Hey, My Man",
sd Louis

            "I aint never
              Left!"

WHERE IS THEM BLACK CLOTHES?

 I know
They got em, some where
in the back, them black suits
 they put on
for the death head
Attack, Them black suits
With the high shiny boots,
I know they already
Got em, or they still being sewed
In the back. So they can put em on
In a snap. Like they jumped out
The Bush bastard's mouth
In the middle of one of his
Bush'it raps. "Attack! Attack!"
A million assholes in black
Is beatin on peoples doors
Like they sellin crack.
Destroyin peoples homes
Like they doin in Iraq
When they put on them black suits,
Them uniforms, they got in
The back, Ready when Bush
Take off presidential grey for
Fuhrer black, them suits

they got in the back, ready
for when Bush really scream
ATTACK! Him, Cheney, Rums
Field and the rest, they already
Gottem, and yo girlfriend the skeeza
Aint cutting no slack, she also
gonna be dressed
In Basic fascist Black

Small Talk in the Mirror

There is some kind of skeleton of ignorant greed
Clutching our ears knows mouth where we breathe
Not you, the other then, the one
Who follows, the one who wont acknowledge
The teeth in your tongue, the stomach in every song
You have sung. Not them, what other grim doppelganger
Wants to hang on your use, prays to our heart that
We demand nothing smart, the fiend of our own living
The one who keep shoving who us you is me them
On toward a valley, an alley, a silly recompense
At your own dumb expense. Say who is the why of our
Lie, the under root of that untruth. Gaggle, babble, tattle,
    rattle, go on
Skedaddle, swim or paddle from clean, be ugly, be mean
Escape, say you weren't on the scene, is ob and un seen, the
    next grim reaper
Is the creature you have made.

RACE OR CLASS?

Race or Class, is the stymieing contradiction
Puzzling those who ponder Affirmative action.
The black middle class, some say, has grown so strong
As to make any social remuneration for that often crass
Betraying bunch redundant, they have already copped
That prize, for which millions of Bloods gave their lives.
And there are white folks poor as dirt, who make even
Some brothers and sisters in the projects look like they doing
    good.
Oh yeh, is our reaction, water climbing up our nervous
    traceries
But slavery still make it plain that black you was and black you
    is
No matter what you gain. So yeh, we must include class
    consideration
So that Colin Powell's boring son do not cop at Little Abner
    Jr.'s expense,
Right on. But I leave you with this burning fact which Du Bois
Was wise enough to state, "Many have suffered as much as we
But none of them was real estate!"

Those who dug Lester Young are not surprised

But those

Who can't understand
What they did, can't understand
Who they are. Are then lost, in the moss, lost to the discourse
Uncorrected, misdirected, uninspected, unprotected,
never seen or known them or they, we and us, all, yall
so then be unknown to most except the host
who told them they ain't who they is
so insist they is who they ain't, its quaint, just add
a little paint, and say the same brain as the insane
and not know, who you, who he, who we, blind like in Spanish
can not si si see. As if race was a waste it is, horse number
    three ain't none of we. And class
was it true, others the same as you, but on your head, if you
upside down, they underground, that's cool, its romantic
you get frantic, they answers antic, like the guy
who crawl up out the bottle and want to know if you got his
    bubble.
But pleas to make you understand, you is another breathing
    space
who got they own time and place. Come this far in a minute.
Ain't even outta breath, come this far so soon, don't know
    yrself

Drunk some coon swoon, 145 years that's a beginndin again
44=08, start in 09 equals the time, and its 10, one again. Come
    so far so quick
They forget to tell you wasn't just slow you wasn't just
    uneducated
You was slick, you wasn't just all heart, you was also very smart.
How you think you was drug over here in chains, next thing
    we know
You the president! God damn, you think you could survive
    amongst this hostile tribe
and not be smart, plus tough, w/ all that heart. Those who
    dug Lester Young
would understand. . . . Wha's happenin, Prez?

Note to Sylvia Robinson from when I saw her walking through the projects in 1966

What beauty is not anomalous
And strange, what love is not
In danger and fragile, what goodness
Is not sometimey and sweet, what grand
Joyousness not shy and seeming incomplete
We are what we can be together never enough
Though without each other we don't know our selves
And would spend the rest of our days looking over our
Shoulder at where we thought we saw ourselves
Crossing another street.

MISSISSIPPI GODDAMN!

There are some negroes
Who will always be
Negroes unless they turn into
Something worse.
There are some negroes who will always be
Niggers, there are some negroes who will always
Be slaves, coons, jiggaboos, woogies, any thing but
Men and women able to think and understand
How we have been dismantled in this land.
I saw Hillary Clinton in Mississippi with two giant coons
One on each side, like Mandrake the Magician
With her own two Lothars . . . But by now, how could
This cow lie, has slavery been so obscured, has that evil
Been so cured, that two mindless swinish wooden negroes
Could help the slavemasters mistress repeal the emancipation.
Is this the meaning of integration or the effects of segregation.
That we would rather guard capitalism's whore than struggle
For ourselves and with ourselves to achieve something more.

Comfortable w/ intelligence

Inspired
 by consciousness
made bold by
 human grandeur
Why is it
 so much dumb stuff
 grows up around you?
There is that space
of breathing of heart beat
going in & out
that gives access
to questions, wrong answers
alcoholic fits
distances of misunderstanding
like the zoo of incompatible
blindness, like correspondences
of pain, propositions
of ill lurking
parades of falseness,
maledict outright
lies, whys to protect
the unwise, suits against
directness, litigation against
openness, distortions

bad thinking, stalling
mumbles, castigated light
Even so, we are comfortable
w/ revelation, inspired
by brilliant conversation
raised up by the mention
of intelligence, the longing for
poetry of knowing, of doing
of actual meaning,
when & where it is
anyway, despite the
remarkable stupidity
that encases the world
in repetitious
boring
        tragedy

PRESCRIPTION DRUG

Rush, Limp Balls &
His ass –ociate,
The Lizard, run a
Dumb show w/they boy
The Chain, Which mean
Steal links in his head
Instead of a Brain!
Too Dumb to be graduate
Racists, they are still
Studying Ugly but
Seem to have succeeded
In their seedy aspiration.
The three in mufti
Like the GOP trying
To become the Klan
Not trying, being, instead
The KKK
Krazy Korny Ksuckers
Whose IQ collectively is
Minus 8, whose
Conversation is masturbation
w/ early Neanderthal
Accent, not smart
Neanderthals but

The dumb ones.
And don't forget the
Fish egg Karl
Who is what feces
Becomes if not flushed
Away he wants to stay
Like the chain, Oh,
Slave Memory!, in the
News as old &
Smelling like dead bodies
Turning into mere odor.
Shd we ignore them?
We shd not only deplore
Them, but insist they
Be questioned, as I
Shd have been when
I made the Zionists angry.
Yes, they need to be
Summoned to court
To explain the issue
& what is they point.
There must be a place
A time, when racism
Is a crime. where if
The answers smack
Of smack, not fact
You get time for yr slime.
Perhaps we shd
Summon them to a
People's Tribunal
Ok, Scream "Don't Glorify
The Urinal!"
So let thousands have

A chance to ask what
They meant, where are their
Facts, & I will submit
To the same. Murdoch
Too for his ugly cartoon
Showing Obama slain
By two cops! We need
An assembly, a gathering
Of the people to
Ask questions of them,
Of us, of myself.
What are you talking about?
What do you mean?
And judge, let the grass
Roots judge- & we will
Go from there Yeh-
What are you saying?
What do you mean?
& Where are the facts?

ALL SONGS ARE CRAZY

Some are beautiful.
Who could sing
All the songs we know?
How many of us that can, know
How many of those who sing know
What singing is.
So I who have sung and have heard song
Want to know the singers
And the song
I who have learned singing from the oldest singers
In the world and have sung some songs myself
Want to create that song that everybody knows
And that everybody will sing one day.
So what is left to do? That is how the song
Begins.

I'm Not Fooled

This is still Slavery
Not fooled at all
This is still slavery
Even with OBAMA, I'M STILL NOT FOOLED
THIS IS STILL SLAVERY, NOT FOOLED AT ALL
IF IT WASN'T SLAVERY OBAMA COULD FIGHT BACK
HE'S DONE THINGS, GOOD THINGS, BUT
I'M STILL NOT FOOLED, THIS IS STILL SLAVERY.
So what you gonna act like Miles, tellin me "So What?"
Out yr brains closed mouth, and on the open streets
Not only so what but bump me, chump me, chump us all, you say
Actin like Miles but you aint Miles, you the dressed up slave
    master ghost
Just as you always was. I ain't fooled. It's still slavery still is still
    is. I aint fooled
Excuse me
The fone ringing.

The New Invasion of Africa

So it wd be this way
That they wd get a negro
To bomb his own home
To join with the actual colonial
Scum, Britain, France, add Poison Hillary
With Israel and the Saudi to make certain
That revolution in Africa must have a stopper
So call in the white Euro people who long tasted our blood
They would be the copper, overthrow Libya
With some bullshit humanitarian scam
With the negro yapping to make it seem right (far right)
But that's how Africa got enslaved by the white
A negro selling his own folk, delivering us to slavery
In the middle of the night.
When will you learn poet
And remember it so you know it
Imperialism can look like anything
Can be quiet and intelligent and even have
A pretty wife. But in the end, it is insatiable
And if it needs to, it will take your life.

WHAT'S THAT WHO IS THIS IN THEM OLD NAZI CLOTHES? NAZI'S DEAD

I thought. I thought they said all them Nazis was outta here
    permanent.
I remember 20 years ago I came into the city from the
    Holland tunnel and the vibe was strong
I wrote, "I feel Nazis. There's Nazi's here." And through
The years I wd say it again sometimes pointing out specific
    things and vibes and even Creepus Dungus
Like Rudy the Vile or Dubya the international murderer. But
    these
Were in government, so when they left you breathed easier.
    But now
These killers are not in the government, they say they don't
    like the government
that they enemies of the government. But what does that
Mean. It means you can't unelect them. Send them home to
    Texas to help vegetate the crops?
And who are these brazens beings? They say they are people.
They have the law on their side, saying they are humans just
    like us. But
I saw a sign at the Occupy said if the Corporations are Human
I wanna see Texas execute one! Then we'll be sure. But not
    now, this
Human cry is just a dumb ass lie, and you a fool to go for it!
    They are big time mechanized

Telecommunicated gangs, whose sole purpose is to squeeze us
for maximum profit. That's their only reason, no matter with
murder and treason. They send jobs to poor countries for
criminal
Pay, somebody call you for your phone bill, ask them where
    they from, India they say, not the Bronx.
Look in your clothes, at those labels, for those jobs that they
    stole. Squeezing throats all over the
world to make you unemployed and spread poverty
    throughout the world. It is not a coincidence
That Wall Street was a plantation. Now they want to run the
    whole nation. Not as Weise Ubermensch
The White Superman, with Adolph at the helm, but still as
Fascist dictatorship, Superpacs, the Corpses uber alles. Not as
government but over government, in place of government.
Their leaders are Romneys, Rome's knees. New Caesars on
an International throne. On our knees before Rome again.
Not with little Charlie Chaplin mustaches and easily satirized
struts to force us into gas chambers and concentration camps,
Just Buy! Sell! Completely Free (shudder when you hear
them say that word) Free! to squander our lives for their
gain. Paying no taxes, new mixmatch Himmlers like Tom Ass
Clarence and his criminal wife praying to their non existent
God which they count as they step through the blood giggling
"Citizens United" the scalding song of vampires mumbling
all over the world as they come to evict us from our homes
and our schools, public education is on their hit list as well.
Whether you speak Spanish or Greek whether it comes out of
Christies mouth or Booker's, Bloomberg or some other Freak.

This the new anti fascist war we must fight, Against the rule of the Corpses. The Corporate Dictatorship forming in front of our eyes. It can no longer surprise. Get your pitch forks ready. Strike Hard and True. You get them or they get you.

SUPPOSE YOU BELIEVED THAT

All this pain is necessary
And that you had gotten
Many awards saying you copped
Because you can suffer
Like a mimmy jimmy, better
Than most
And that you would receive
A reward, up stairs, in the
Upper Room, when you got to Hebin
Hebin, and when the time came to split
So you cd finally get your reward
What you heard instead is a voice
Coming from the top of the Empire
State building, Chump, Chump, chump
Then whatchu gonna do, this time, Bayyyyy
Beee . . . Chump, Chump, Chump

Ballad Air & Fire

for Sylvia or Amina

There is music
sometimes
in lonely
shadows
blue music
sometimes
purple music
black music
red music
but these are left from crowds
of people
listening and singing
from generation
to generation

All the civilizations humans have built
(speed us up we look like ants)
our whole lives lived in an inch
or two. And those few seconds
that we breathe

in that incredible speed
blurs of sight and sound
the wind's theories

So for us to have been together, even
for this moment
profound like a leaf
blown in the wind

to have been together
and known you, and despite our pain
to have grasped much of what joy exists
accompanied by the ring and peal of your
romantic laughter

is what it was about, really. Life.
Loving someone, and struggling

INDEX